Judeo-Persian Writings

Introducing Judeo-Persian writings, this original collection gives parallel samples in Judeo-Persian and Perso-Arabic script and translations in English. Judeo-Persian writings not only reflect the twenty-seven centuries of Jewish life in Iran, but they are also a testament to their intellectual, cultural, and socioeconomic conditions.

Such writings, found in the forms of verse or prose, are flavored with Judaic, Iranian and Islamic elements. The significant value of Judeo-Persian writing is found in the areas of linguistics, history and sociocultural and literary issues. The rhetorical forms and literary genres of epic, didactic, lyric and satirical poetry can be a valuable addition to the rich Iranian literary tradition and poetical arts. Also, as a Judaic literary contribution, the work is a representation of the literary activity of Middle Eastern Jews not so well recognized in Judaic global literature.

This book is a comprehensive introduction to the rich literary tradition of works written in Judeo-Persian and also serves as a guide to transliterate many other significant Judeo-Persian works that have not yet been transliterated into Perso-Arabic script. The collection will be of value to students and researchers interested in history, sociology and Iranian and Jewish studies.

Nahid Pirnazar teaches Judeo-Persian literature and the history of Iranian Jews at UCLA and is the founder of House of Judeo-Persian Manuscripts. Her recent publications include: *Fārsihood* (2018), "Voluntary Conversions of Iranian Jews in the Nineteenth Century", *Iran Namg* (2019) and *Ketāb-e Anūsi* (2020).

Iranian Studies

Edited by: Homa Katouzian

University of Oxford

and

Mohamad Tavakoli

University of Toronto

Since 1967 the International Society for Iranian Studies (ISIS) has been a leading learned society for the advancement of new approaches in the study of Iranian society, history, culture, and literature. The new ISIS Iranian Studies series published by Routledge will provide a venue for the publication of original and innovative scholarly works in all areas of Iranian and Persianate Studies.

Persian Literature and Modernity
Production and Reception
Edited by Hamid Rezaei Yazdi and Arshavez Mozafari

Rival Conceptions of Freedom in Modern Iran
An Intellectual History of the Constitutional Revolution
Ahmad Hashemi

Iran and Palestine
Past, Present, Future
Seyed Ali Alavi

Persian Calligraphy
A Corpus Study of Letterforms
Mahdiyeh Meidani

Iranian National Cinema
The Interaction of Policy, Genre, Funding and Reception
Anne Démy-Geroe

Judeo-Persian Writings
A Manifestation of Intellectual and Literary Life
Edited and Compiled by Nahid Pirnazar

For more information about this series, please visit: www.routledge.com/middleeaststudies/series/IRST

Judeo-Persian Writings

A Manifestation of Intellectual and Literary Life

Edited and Compiled by
Nahid Pirnazar

Routledge
Taylor & Francis Group
LONDON AND NEW YORK

First published 2022
by Routledge
2 Park Square, Milton Park, Abingdon, Oxon OX14 4RN

and by Routledge
52 Vanderbilt Avenue, New York, NY 10017

Routledge is an imprint of the Taylor & Francis Group, an informa business

British Library Cataloguing-in-Publication Data
A catalogue record for this book is available from the British Library

Library of Congress Cataloging-in-Publication Data
A catalog record for this book has been requested

ISBN: 978-1-032-14576-1 (hbk)
ISBN: 978-0-367-50747-3 (pbk)
ISBN: 978-1-003-03174-1 (ebk)

DOI: 10.4324/9781003031741

Typeset in Times New Roman
by Apex CoVantage, LLC

Dedicated to my husband, Jeffrey Oberman, who has always encouraged and supported my academic achievements.

Also to my daughters, Shireen and Jasmine, for their unconditional love, help and support.

Contents

Acknowledgments

The publication of this book would not have been possible without the support, encouragement and assistance of a number of individuals.

First and foremost, I am indebted to my mentors, the late Prof. Hossein Ziai, the late Prof. Amnon Netzer and Prof. William Schniedwind, who were all members of my doctoral committee at UCLA. I will always value the encouragement, academic teachings and guidance they gave to me over the years.

My appreciation is also extended to the following:

All my students, throughout the years, that I have taught Judeo-Persian text and literature. It has been their input, assistance and suggestions that have resulted in the book that you now see. It is my hope that this book will benefit all other students and scholars interested in the subject matter of this book.

Mrs. Jenny Massaband for Persian word processing and editing, Mr. Nejat Yaghubi for his assistance in transliterations and reviewing all the lines written in Judeo-Persian. My two dedicated interns, Sepideh Yadidsion and Tania Yaghobian, for Hebrew word processing and editing.

Dr. George W. Maschke for the initial review of the English translation of the poetry.

Prof. Ahmad Karimi-Hakkak for the final review of the entire book and the final corrections of the English translations of the poetry.

Prof. Mohamad Tavakoli, chief editor of *Iran-Namag*, for his unlimited support and directions leading to the publication of this book.

Figures and tables

Figures

Tables

Part I

Formation and history of Judeo-Persian

1 An overview of Iranian Jewish intellectual history

Introduction

The literature of a nation can be looked upon as an embellished first-hand account of the history by which people's lives, thoughts and feelings have been reflected throughout the ages. The study of Judeo-Persian manuscripts, similar to an archaeological investigation, provides the tools to discover the hidden culture and history of the Iranian Jews, as well as their intellectual life. It acknowledges the endeavors of a people who were neglected and forgotten throughout the centuries in a country where they lived in for over twenty-seven centuries. Hence, their proper position in Iranian history and literature can be revealed and acknowledged.

Judeo-Persian script, meaning writings in Hebrew letters in the Persian language, recorded the intellectual history and the literary writings of Iranian Jews until the first two decades of the 20th century. Such documents demonstrate the dual Iranian national and Jewish identity of Iranian Jewry by sharing the same distinctive traditions, culture, and language. Recent discoveries of Judeo-Persian writings in Afghanistan and Geniza or those previously found outside the borders of contemporary Iran depict the vast demographic spread of Iranian Jews within the greater Iranian community. Through their intellectual and literary contributions, Judeo-Persian authors have also had a share in the development of Iranian heritage. By choosing to write and record their works in the Judeo-Persian script, they have at the same time maintained their religious identity as Jews, which otherwise might have faded. Ever since the Authoritative Center, *Resh Galuta*, was moved from Babylonia to Andolesia (915 C.E.), Iranian Jews had gradually lost their familiarity with the Hebrew language and their Judaic legacy. Except for those literate in Hebrew and biblical writings, reading about their religious heritage in Judeo-Persian certainly played an important role in the preservation of lay people's Jewish identity.

Having lived as a religious minority throughout centuries, the religious minorities of Iran turned a new page with the adoption of Iranian Constitution

DOI: 10.4324/9781003031741-2

(1909 C.E.), giving them a new sociocultural life. Now recognized as Iranian citizens, at least in terms of the laws governing the country, Jews were no longer confined to Jewish quarters and schools. Civil rights and a national system of education offered the Jews command of Perso-Arabic script. This new freedom empowered their Iranian national identity and influenced many to put the use of Judeo-Persian aside. By the second half of the 20th century, the array of Judeo-Persian works was left untouched at individual archives or on the shelves of world libraries, giving Iranian Jews little chance to share their cultural contributions with the rest of Iranians in Perso-Arabic script.

Historical background of Iranian Jewry

Historically, Jews settled in Iran and other areas later considered a part of the Iranian Empire on four significant occasions. The first occasion was after the fall of Israel in B.C.E. 744, when the Israelites were relocated by the Assyrian Empire to Nineveh. The second occasion was when the Jews who had already been brought in as captives to Babylonia by Nebuchadnezzar in B.C. 586 were freed by Cyrus the Great in B.C.E. 539. The third occasion was after the destruction of the Second Temple (70 C.E.), which was followed by the compilation of the Babylonian Talmud. The fourth occasion was after the Spanish expulsion during the Safavid era (1501–1736 C.E.), when the Sephardic Jews of Ottoman Turkey were relocated from Georgia to Farahabad on the southern shores of the Caspian Sea and later to other parts of Iran. It is worth noting that, contrary to many of the later residents of Iran, including the Arabs and the Turks who entered the land through invasions, Jews came either as captives, who were set free in Iran, or voluntary immigrants.

The first Israelites, who were relocated to Nineveh (II Kings 15–29, 17:6; 1 Chronicles 5:2), became known as the Ten Lost Tribes. They lived in territories first ruled by the Assyrians, but after the defeat of the Assyrians by an alliance of the Medes and Babylonians (B.C.E. 612–610, Jeremiah: 51:11–12, 28), the territories were annexed to Iran (Horn 1999, 190–193). The annexation occurred because of an agreement between the Medes and Babylonians whereby the Medes took the northern territories, which included Nineveh, and the Babylonians took the rest of Mesopotamia and the western territories.

The second occasion was followed by the rise of the Achaemenid dynasty in Iran (B.C.E. 559–331), known as the Persian Period. This period has left a lasting legacy on Jewish history as well as the Jews of Iran. During this period, the Jews were granted a great amount of religious autonomy, resulting in opportunities for prosperity. The Jews were offered the option to live in Babylonia or move back to Jerusalem. Those Jews who remained in Babylonia gradually moved eastward to Lar, Khuzestan, Shush, Pasargadae and finally Isfahan (Netzer 1996b, 13).

Recognized as a liberator, Cyrus had high hopes of rebuilding the Temple for the Jews. Unfortunately, he did not live long enough to fulfill this plan. Years later, this mission was finally accomplished by his son-in-law and the major general of his army, Dariush I (B.C.E. 522–486). The Second Temple, built between the years of B.C.E. 520 and 516, became the symbol of Iranian presence in Jerusalem (Purvis 1999, 218–219).

The third occasion of Jewish migration to Iran following the destruction of the Second Temple in 70 C.E. by the Romans resulted in the expansion of Jewish academies in Babylonia and lured many Jewish scholars who for centuries had worked on the interpretation of Mishna, codified Jewish law, and compilation of the Babylonian Talmud in the diaspora. In Babylonia, the Talmud, "the most timeless of religious works was composed, perfected and presented, as a legacy to the Jewish world", during the early part of the Sasanian period (Levy 1999, 132). Jacob Neusner, a scholar of the Sasanian era, states that: "While the Jews of the Parthian and Sasanian empires spoke (Eastern) Aramaic, not Middle Persian, Persian influence on Judaism through the Babylonian Talmud (Bavli) is by no means negligible" (Neusner 2005, 347–350).[1]

Also, as Habib Levy suggests, considering the facts that the Babylonian Talmud was composed on Iranian soil and that the religious scholars compiling it had communication with the Sasanian court and polemics with the Zoroastrian scholars, the "Babylonian Talmud could be considered the Iranian Talmud" (Levy, 1999, 133).

Throughout the pre-Islamic era, Iranian Jews were to maintain dual allegiance to their Iranian and Jewish identities (Berquist 1995, 42). The loyalty of Iranian Jews to both their religious ethnicity and their new self-elected homeland can be seen throughout the history of the region. Such relations date back to the influence of the prophets Daniel, Haggai and Zechariah in the Iranian courts, as well as the mission of Zerubabel for the rebuilding of the Second Temple from the Iranian treasury (B.C.E. 520–515). Furthermore, the impact of the dual role of Ezra and Nehemiah as Jews and Iranian agents in the expansion and reconstruction of the city of Jerusalem speaks of the place of Iranians in the royal court. In fact, it was a tradition during the Persian period to make sacrifices for the health and prosperity of the shah of Iran and the royal family at the altar (Tadmor 1976, 171–172; Ezra, 6:11).

However, Iranian culture did not begin to permeate into the Jewish community until the early Sassanid era. Influenced by the friendly relationships

1 For details, see: Shai Secunda. 2014. *The Iranian Talmud, Reading the Bavli in Its Sasanian Context*. Philadelphia: 2014; *Shoshannat Yasskov* 2012, edited by Shai Secunda and Steven Fine. Leiden and Boston: E.J. Brill.

maintained by the Jewish Academies and Shapur I and II, Rabbi Yossi (d. 323 C.E.), the religious leader of Jews in the diaspora, recommended that Jews learn to speak the language of the land (Netzer 1996b, 42). Iranian Jews, who at the time spoke Eastern Aramaic, gradually began speaking Middle Persian and later New Persian. The existence of numerous Middle Persian (Pahlavi) terms in the Talmudic texts is evidence of such linguistic acculturation. In the same era, Iranian Jewish soldiers are reported to have fought against the Romans as a part of the Iranian army (Netzer 1996b, 34–35). Rabbi Yossi's recommendation laid the foundation for the Iranian Jewish cultural identity, which would give birth to the vast literary contributions of Judeo-Persian literature: something unique for Iranian Jews to identify themselves with.

Medieval Jewish contributors to Iranian intellectual identity

The list of Jews contributing to the development of Iranian heritage and, ultimately, Iranian intellectual identity from antiquity to modern times is extensive. While most of the authors wrote their work in Judeo-Persian in the medieval era, one may find their contributions recorded in Perso-Arabic script as well.

Sa'd b. Manṣūr Ibn Kammūna (1215–1284) was a 13th-century Jewish physician (ophthalmologist), philosopher and critic of religion. He was born in a Jewish family and "he must have received a thorough education in both Jewish and Islamic letters", as is evident from his sophistication in both fields (Pourjavady & Schmidtke 2006, 8). His most significant contribution to the history of philosophy is his detailed commentary on Suhrawardi's *al-Talwiḥat,* completed in 1268, in which he conveys essential points of the Illumination Philosophy (Pourjavady & Schmidtke 2006, 10). His conversion to Islam has been the subject of argument by different bibliographers at different times. Although some experts, like Moritz Steinschneider, believe that Ibn Kammūna converted to Islam, some of the great pioneers of Judeo-Arabic studies, notably D.H. Baneth, have opposed that assumption. Pourjavady and Schmidtke have also argued against his conversion in their very recent book-length study (Pourjavady & Schmidtke 2006, 22; Stanford Encyclopedia of Philosophy, S.V. "Ibn Kammūna"; Jewish Virtual Library, S.V. "Ibn Kammūna").[2]

Further evidence of Ibn Kammūna's Jewish ties is his controversial treatise and his arguments on the three monotheistic religions. His devotion to Judaism is beyond doubt in the *Tanqiḥ* (*Examination of the Three Faiths*), a

2 www.google.com/search?client=firefox-b-1-d&q=www.+Jewishvirtuallibrary.org+Ibn+Kammuna (Accessed June, 2020)

remarkable work of its time period completed in 1280 and a work for which he was persecuted four years later (Pourjavady & Schmidtke 2006, 16).

Sa'd al-Dowleh and **Rashīd al-Dīn Fażl–Allāh** were two Iranian statesmen. During the Ilkhanid period (1258–1295), before the new rulers had converted to Islam, the Iranian Jews achieved their greatest prominence in public life in Iran, never to be repeated again. Within these fifty years, Jews were able to attain a certain degree of acculturation to the larger Iranian community. As a result, they obtained high positions in the empire as court officials, physicians, astronomers and, above all, political leaders, *viziers* of the great Mongol Persian Empire (Fischel 1949, 824). Through his wisdom and expertise, the Jewish court physician Sa'd al-Dowleh gained the confidence of Arghun Khān (1284–1291). Along with valuing his medical expertise, Arghun Khān approached him for his advice on fiscal matters in Baghdad (Fischel, 1949, 97–98), where he was eventually appointed controller of the *Divan* and chief of the financial administration. In recognition of his services to the state later that year (1289), Arghun appointed him chief of the entire administration, first minister and *vizier* over all the countries of his empire (Fischel 1949, 100–103).

The other Jewish physician and politician of the early Ilkhanid era was Rashid al-Din Fażllolah (b. 1247) from Hamedan, who is confirmed to have converted to Islam in 1278, when his name was changed (Spuler 1939, 247–249) from Rashid al-Dowleh to Rashid al-din, as Netzer reports from Spuler (Netzer 1994, 119).

According to the sources, Rashid al-Din was not only the greatest scholar of his time and a wealthy man but also an ingenious politician. He achieved the highest administrative rank, as grand *vizier*, in 1298, by Ghāzan Khān (1295–1304) and in 1312 by Uljaytu (1304–1316). In that capacity, Rashid al-Din built schools, hospitals and other public educational institutions in the suburb of Tabriz. He named this little town, inhabited by intellectuals and artists, Rab'-e Rashidi (Netzer 1994, 118–119, 123). Rashid al-Din's rapid rise in politics derived from his unique scholarly achievements. With his numerous Persian-language treatises on medical and scholarly subjects, he made the newly founded capital of Soltaniyeh a respected center of learning in the Islamic world. His most important work, *Jami' al-tawārikh* (*Comprehensive History*), in several volumes and completed in 1302, is the first disciplined study of the history of all nations of the known world (Levy 1999, 246).

(An Anthology of the Persian Poetry of the Jews of Iran)

Sa'īd **Sarmad Kāshāni** was a Persian mystic and poet born to a priestly family in Kashan in the early 17th century. He was a man of great intellect and knowledge who seemed to have mastered the Hebrew language and rabbinical literature. Sarmad's life started as a Jew in Kashan, where he was born into a "family of learned Yahuds, of a class whom they call Rabbanim"

(*School of Manners* 1901, trans. 299). In his quest for divine truth, Sarmad converted to Islam at about the age of twenty-five in 1615.[3]

Nevertheless, he did not find the answer to his inquiries in his new religious training, nor in the philosophical discussions he had participated in as a student between renowned scholars of his time, Mulla Sadra and Abul Qasim Mir Fendereski (Gupta 1991, 3). Sarmad thus migrated to India in hopes of finding answers to his spiritual questions. Ultimately, in 1661, at the age of seventy, his destiny was to be executed on the steps of Jame‘ Mosque in Delhi far from his native land, Iran (Fischel 1948–49, 160–172).

As a humanist, a *Ṣufi* and a poet, Sarmad started his literary work in India in the Persian language. There, he is mainly regarded as a *Ṣufi* or a saint who used Persian poetry as a means of communication. However, Walter Fischel perceives Sarmad as someone who "entered the annals of Persian literature as a composer of Persian *Ṣerce* poetry" (Fischel 1948–49, 161). In the meantime, Fażl Mahmud Asiri, professor of Urdu and Islamic studies, values Sarmad as someone who contributed to Indian intellectual life. He believes that Sarmad's quatrains "were preserved and treated as the sacred relics of a great martyr in India" (Asiri 1950, ii). In general, Sarmad's lifestyle, philosophy and works have had various influences upon Judaism, Indian culture and Iranian literature.

Development and characteristics of Judeo-Persian

As an account of the heritage of Iranian Jewry, Judeo-Persian literature not only represents the sentiments and mentality of its authors but also reflects certain elements specific to its Iranian Jewish identity. Except in some individual cases, the literature of Iranian Jews written in Judeo-Persian had not received scholarly attention until the 19th century for different reasons. Among such reasons are the nature of the writings, which caused a self-imposed isolation, as well as the socioeconomic conditions of its authors and readers. In spite of all the previous elements, as Jan Rypka states, "it is a curious coincidence that the earliest records in the Persian language are at the same time the earliest records of Judeo-Persian literature" (Rypka 1968, 737).

3 Fazl Mahmud Asiri. 1991. "Rubaiyat-e Sarmad", in *Visva- Baharati 11* (Santiniketan: Visva-Baharati, 1950), iv. Asiri confirms the conversion before his departure from Iran but does not mention a date. M.G. Gupta, in *Sarmad, The Saint,* gives the date of 1615 for his conversion: see M.G. Gupta, *Sarmad, the Saint: Life and Works*. Agra: MG Publishers, 2.
Muhsin Fānī. 1262. *Dabistan al Mazahib.* Trans. 1846. Bombay.
For further details on Sarmad, his life and work, see: Nahid Pirnazar, "Sarmad of Kashan: Jewish Saint, Persian Poet", *Iran Namg*, vol. 1, no. 3 (Fall 2016).

Although individual attempts had started before, the scope of the revival of Judeo-Persian studies in Europe was widened after the visit of Elkan Nathan Adler to Iran in the late 19th century. Adler, a Jewish scholar and collector of Judaic documents, visited Tehran, Samarkand and Bukhara in 1896, where he examined and purchased a large amount of Judeo-Persian manuscripts. In an article entitled "The Persian Jews: Their Books and Their Ritual", Adler gave a detailed description of the manuscripts he had acquired. It was Adler's collection of manuscripts used by Wilhelm Bacher, a Jewish rabbi from Budapest, who over the next two decades researched, published and commented upon the documents. As a part of his studies, Bacher published in 1907 a work on two of the most prominent Judeo-Persian poets—namely Shāhin (13th–14th century), a contemporary of Soltan Abu Saeed (1316–1335), and 'Emrāni (15th–16th century), born in 1454.

With some exceptions, however, modern-day European scholars have focused mainly on Judeo-Persian studies from a linguistic perspective and as a subcategory of Judaic literature. Even when studied through literary analysis, the documents are still regarded as a part of Jewish literary works. *An Anthology of the Persian Poetry of the Jews of Iran*, edited by Amnon Netzer in 1973, takes the first step in introducing the works of the Persian-speaking Jews of Iran in the Persian literary tradition.

Similar to any other literary work, the cultural background, religious pressures and socioeconomic condition of Iranian Jews should be taken into consideration in the evaluation of Judeo-Persian literature to justify the general lack of refined language and development of intellectual concepts. Yet exceptions to the rule exist, and many fine literary works are found in Judeo-Persian in terms of style, language and content. Critics of Judeo-Persian literature should be reminded that the survival of the dual Iranian Jewish identity, especially after the Arab invasion, was mainly made possible by the Jews being anchored in a balanced and continuous use of both Persian language and culture, as well as the practice of Jewish cultural traditions.

Definition of Judeo-Persian

Judeo-Persian is a Persian language, from the late Middle Persian textual tradition to New Persian, written in Hebrew characters. The content of Judeo-Persian writings may range from classical literary works to regional poetry or prose. Except for some printings of the documents in the early 20th century, most texts are handwritten in manuscripts.

In order to fully grasp the idiosyncrasies of Judeo-Persian literature, one must comprehend the Iranian Jews' preference for the Hebrew script over the Perso-Arabic script. The motivation for writing in Hebrew script could simply have been for the practical reason of sharing the script of the Torah, a text they were already familiar with. Moreover, scholars like Gilbert Lazard suggest that "the employment of Perso-Arabic script of the Koran, by the Jews was considered as a sign of breaching religious loyalty, conversion, and act of betrayal" (Lazard 1971, 429–432; Fischel 1971, 432–439).

Judeo-Persian writings are found in the form of verse or prose flavored with Judaic, Iranian and Islamic elements. Thematically, they cover religious or secular contents. The intended readership of Judeo-Persian writings is limited to Persian-speaking Jews literate in Hebrew characters. In general, a large intellectual gap is noticeable between the intended audience and the authors of Judeo-Persian literature. Judeo-Persian authors were found to be intellectually far more sophisticated than their audience and equally influenced by non-Iranian Jews as well as non-Jewish Iranians. As Amnon Netzer reports, the list includes:

Maimonides (Egypt, 1135–1204; Bahia Ibn Pekuda (Spain, 11th century); Isrāel ben Negārā (Israel, 1555–1628); Sa'diā Gāon (Egypt/Babylonia, 882–942); Shlomo Ibn Gebirol (Spain, 1025–1065); Yehudā Halevy (Spain, 1085–1141); Shemu'el ben 'Abbās (North Africa, 12th century); Rabbi Shim'un ben Gamliel and Abraham ibn Ḥasadai (Spain, 13th century).

As for non-Jewish Iranians, Netzer lists poets like:

> Ferdowsi (935–c.1020/126); Neẓāmī Ganjavi (c. 1130/41–1209); Khayyām (1048–1131); 'Obayd-e Zākāni (1300–1371); Sheykh Farīd al-Din 'Attar (c. 1145–c. 1221); Jalāl al-Din Mowlavi, also known as Rumi (13th century); Sa'di (1210–1292) and Hāfeẓ (1315–1390) (Netzer 1996a 52–97; 1999a 125–136).

In some cases, Hebrew poetry paraphrased, translated or as part of a poetic device has also been represented in Judeo-Persian literary writings (Netzer 1996a, 96–97).

The revival of Judeo-Persian studies

An investigation of pioneer researchers and contemporary Judeo-Persian scholars demonstrates the accomplishments already achieved in the field of linguistics and Judaic religious and literary works. Except for the past few decades, not much attention was given to the study of Judeo-Persian, its cultural aspects and inputs, nor to the place of Judeo-Persian writings in the stream of traditional Persian literature. Professor Amnon Netzer's *Montakhab-e Ash'ār-e Fārs ī az Ā sār-e Yahūdīyān-e Irān*, published in Persian in 1973, can be considered the first work in this respect. Fortunately, in recent years, we find Judeo-Persian scholarly works in the area received from Iran in the cities of Tehran, Quom and Hamedan.

Some of the pioneering Judeo-Persian scholars of modern studies, whose contributions to the field should be acknowledged, as Yerushalmi lists them

(Yeroushalmi 1995, 5), include Professor K.D. Hassler, who translated *The Song of Songs* in 1829; Solomon Munk, who published the Judeo-Persian version of Sa'diā Gāon's *Isaiah* in 1838 and Paul de Lagarde, who published *Persische Studien* in 1884 to examine the essential features of Judeo-Persian literature and linguistics for the first time (De Lagarde 1884, 68–69). Elkan Nathan Adler was a "bibliophile and scholar of Jewish material", who visited Tehran, Bukhara and Samarkand, collecting manuscripts, in 1897. Adler's collection brought from the Middle East and Central Asia was an indispensable contribution to Judeo-Persian literature in modern studies (Netzer 1985,11). Professor Wilhelm Bacher, a student of classical Persian literature from Budapest (d. 1913), by working on the collections of Adler in 1907, introduces the rich background of of Judeo-Persian poetry to the West, including two of its most prominent poets, Shāhīn and 'Emrānī. Among other scholars, the names of Theodor Noldeke, Carl Salemann and Paul Horn, who also studied Judeo-Persian texts from a philological point of view, should also be mentioned (Yeroushalmi 1995, 5). The list of contemporary Judeo-Persian scholars includes Jes P. Asmussen from Denmark; Gilbert Lazard from France; Shaul Shaked, Amnon Netzer, Michael Zand and David Yeroushalmi from Israel and Herbert Paper and Vera Bach Moreen from the United States.

Classification of Judeo-Persian writings

Judeo-Persian writings can be classified from different viewpoints. While Gilbert Lazard uses chronological criteria to classify Judeo-Persian writings, Amnon Netzer divides Judeo-Persian works chronologically, thematically and stylistically. With a brief reference to the thematic variations, Lazard, in "The Dialectology of Judeo-Persian", reported by Amnon Netzer, divides Judeo-Persian writings into four periods (Netzer 1996a, 48–52):

1. The oldest group (8th–11th century): including a few disparate articles, private inscriptions or documents.
2. Works from early times (12th–early 14th century): including exegesis of the Bible, translations and commentaries, dictionaries and further extensive material that needs to be further researched.
3. Literary classical Persian (14th–18th century): Judeo-Persian literature blooming after the prosperous secular atmosphere of the early Ilkhānīd period. This era includes works of the most prominent poets and the large bulk of the prose manuscripts.
4. Writings stemming from Bukhara (end of 17th throughout 19th century): including mostly the writings of the Jews in Samarqand and Bukhara during that period.

Netzer's two chronological periods of pre-Mongol with linguistic value and post-Mongol with literary value are divided into two major forms of verse and prose thematically. The thematic variations in the form of verse include: 1) epic works: with biblical, apocryphal, midrashic and historical themes; 2) lyric works: with variations of romantic and mystic themes and 3) didactic works based on Judaic and Iranian ethics and aphoristic literature, as well as oral sources (Netzer 1996a, 52–96). The thematic variations in the form of prose include: 1) manuscripts of translations and commentaries called *tafsir*; 2) halakhah; 3) books of liturgy, "Siddurs"; 4) philosophy and theology; 5) Stories, anecdotes and riddles; 6) dream interpretation, geomancy and astrology; 7) Hebrew-Judeo-Persian dictionaries and 8) books on medicine copied in Judeo-Persian (Netzer 1999a, 23–32).

Values of Judeo-Persian writings

Judeo-Persian writings have significant value in the areas of linguistics, history, sociocultural issues and biblical and secular literature.

The linguistic value was first recognized by Western European 19th-century scholars who recognized the importance of Judeo-Persian texts for a better understanding and explanation of New Persian and Iranian philology. Among them is Paul de Lagarde, the German biblical and oriental studies scholar (Yeroushalmi 1995, 5). Professor Gilbert Lazard, of La Sorbonne University, writes in his dialectology of Judeo-Persian that "Persian texts in Hebrew script contain information on dialects which more often, are otherwise not known" (Lazard 1996, 37–38). Judeo-Persian documents maintain a vital role in the study of the transition from Middle Persian to New Persian.

Among the oldest documents of New Persian language belonging to 750–800 C.E. written in Judeo-Persian were *The Letter of Dandan Uiliq* I, discovered in 1901, and the *Letter of Khotan* (also called *The Letter of Dandan Uiliq* II), discovered in 2004. Both letters, found in the vicinity of each other located in the northeast of Khotan in China, reflect Jewish life in those areas at the rise of Islam in the Middle East.[4]

The study of Judeo-Persian manuscripts also reveals certain historical events that happened to Iranian Jewry, which otherwise would not have been discovered. Thus, information about lesser-known areas of Iranian history can be provided between the lines as well. Such historical reports are well reflected in *Ketāb-e Anūsi*, (The Book of the Forced Converts), written by Bābā'i Ben Loṭf and *Ketāb-e Sargozasht Kashan* (The Chronicle of

4 For further details, see Shaul Shaked, "Jews in Khorasan before the Mongol invasion," in *Iran Namag*, edited by Nahid Pirnazar, vol. 1.no. 2: iv–xvi.

Kashan) by his grandson Bābā'i Ben Farhād, with additional lines by Māshiah Ben Refāel. This 17th- to 18th-century account describes the forced conversions exercised on Iranian Jews. Except for some notes on the back of bibles, memoirs of several Armenian priests and travelogues of travelers such as Pietro Della Valle, such information would have remained unknown if it had not been recorded in verse by Bābāi Ben Loṭf and his followers. Transliterating this book into Perso-Arabic script can shed light not only on the dark and unknown history of the Jews but also on some unknown facts about parts of Iranian history.

The study of Judeo-Persian literature can also indirectly display the socioeconomic and sociocultural conditions of Jews and their relations with non-Jews. For example, reading between the lines of both books written by Bābā'i Ben Loṭf and Bābā'i Ben Farhād, we see the acculturation of Iranian Jews to the sociocultural traditions, music and even cuisine of the time. In these books, we find out that in the midst of the Safavid era's forced conversions, women had access to the royal court and were able to get help from the mother of Shah Abbas II (1642–1666 C.E.) for the members of their community. In the same books, we also see the relations maintained between the Jews and the Iranian rulers, as well as the Shi'ite clerics (Netzer 1996a, 68–69).

Other examples that reveal the level of the acculturation of Iranian Jews into Iranian culture are the works of the two prominent poets, Shāhīn and 'Emrāni. Shāhīn uses the Islamic calendar of his time to report the date, mentioning the year and the month in which he finished his epic of *Ardashīrnāmeh* as 733 A.H. in the middle of the month of *Shavval* (Netzer 1973, 177). In the same manner, the poet 'Emrāni in his amplifications within the *Fatḥnāmeh* speaks of the ethnic meals and dishes contemporary to his time, including the covenant meal between the Israelites and Gibionites (Josh, 9:15), such as *qlayeh* and *boghra*, or speaks of dishes flavored with saffron, describing them as *moz'far* dishes ('Emrāni, 70a:11).[5]

In terms of philosophical values, the *Duties of Judah*, written by Rabbi Yehuda Ben El'Azar (1686 C.E.), deals with fundamental principals of Jewish belief and philosophy from a rational perspective. The author's masterful command of the Persian language and literature and knowledge of Arabic, Hebrew and Aramaic not only reflect the author's depth of knowledge but also include reports of the existence of Jewish libraries contemporary to the time of the author, as well as the level of education of the community (Netzer 1995, ii).

Judeo-Persian poetry of the 14th to 17th century portrays a thorough connection of Jews with Iranian literary tradition. With its various rhetorical

5 حَبَش با نخود آب و قلیه برسر   شهنشاهی همه نعمت مزعفر

forms and literary genres of epic, didactic, lyric and satirical poetry, the vast Judeo-Persian literature can be considered a valuable addition to the rich Iranian poetical arts. A large part of the poetry in the form of epics on biblical and apocryphal topics is due to the two prolific poets, Shāhīn in the 14th century and ʻEmrāni in the 15th and early 16th centuries. The versified version of the Pentateuch, *Afarineshnāmeh*, *Musānāmeh*, known as Shāhin *Torah*, and the story of Queen Esther, *Ardashīrnāmeh*, as well as the account of the biblical *Book of Ezrā*, are just a few examples of Shāhīn's contributions to his dual Irano-Judaic identity. ʻEmrāni's *Fatḥnāmeh*, a follow-up to the work of Shāhīn, versifies the books of Conquest, Ruth and Samuel I and II through the ascension of King David to the throne.

Hardly any form of an Iranian epic can be written without reference made to the legendary heroes and locations of the *Shāhnāmeh*, including characters such as Zāl and Bahman or regions such as Zābol (*Fatḥnāmeh*, BZI 60a: 18–18).[6] Iranian epic names are sometimes used in lyric poetry, such as in *Sāqināmeh* by ʻEmrāni, for expressing the transitory aspect of life (Netzer 1996a, 103). Iranian names and titles such as Dārā, Bahrām, Bahman, Zāl, Esfandīyār and Tahamtan are used by the poets to exemplify the righteous heroes and the believers (*Fatḥnāmeh*, BZI 27a:2, 45a:11).[7] In Judeo-Persian epics, often people of non-Iranian nationalities, such as the Turks, Romans and Arabs, as well as certain individuals, such as Alexander in particular, exemplify the image of evil characters and the non-believers (*Fatḥnāmeh*, BZI 60a:15). Among the pre-Islamic Iranian religious references commonly shared by Judeo-Persian poets is the term *farreh*, with its New Persian concept as divine providence, especially with reference to King David (*Fatḥnāmeh*, BZI 293b:1, 316a:1 and 385b:9).[8] ʻEmrāni, in his *Fatḥnāmeh*, refers to the two abridged transformations of *Avestā* named *Zand* and *Pāzand* (*Fatḥnāmeh*, BZI 65a:12–13),[9] as well as the evil personage of *Ahrīman* or *Ahreman* (*Fatḥnāmeh*, BZI 6b:6).[10]

6
که بهر باب شد با زال دشمن   شنیدید ای یلان اسرار بهمن
چه آمد سوی زابل بر سر زال   به بهمن خنده میزد زالِ با یال

7
بروز کین چون زین بر رخش بندم   نیارد جَست رستم از کمندم
بروز رزم چون اسفندیاری   چو رستم هر یکی چابک سواری

8
زفَرّش ما همه آزاد گشتیم   بدین سان فارغ و دلشاد گشتیم
نمی بینی که فرّ شاه دارد   دمار از تخمدان ما در آرد
زفرّ و هیبت داود بود آن   که مشکل ها همه گردید آسان

9
همه با لات و آذر خوی کرده   به طاعت پشت و با بُت خوی کرده
به کفر و کافری دل کرده خرسند   مقید گشته بهرزند و پازند

10
نگردد اهرمن آخر سلیمان   نداند هر سلیمان نطق مرغان

Common Islamic Iranian concepts and inserted mystic episodes, in the form of allegories, as well as the use of mystic metalanguage, are an indication of the Judeo-Persian poet's knowledge of the concepts.

Judeo-Persian poets such as 'Emrāni, Simanṭov Melamed, Rāqeb and Yusof-e Yahudi have made an attempt to use such concepts. As examples, we can take a look in the *Fatḥnāmeh* of 'Emrāni for such cases. Terms such as *ḥejāb*, "cover or a barrier", for the poet to join the divine truth, are used (*Fatḥnāmeh*, BZI 6b:8, 12).[11] Terms used by the poets such as: *dām va dāneh*, "trap and seed" (*Fatḥnāmeh*, BZI 5a:9) and[12] *qafas*, "cage" (*Fatḥnāmeh*, BZI 5a:13,16),[13] as well as the use of *Ṭūṭi*, "parrot" (*Fatḥnāmeh*, BZI 5a:1, 10a:19)[14] and the legendary images similar to the phoenix, such as *Sīmorq* or *'Anqā* (*Fatḥnāmeh*, BZI 11a:4, 54b:4)[15] are all indications of the poet's connections to the Iranian literary metalanguage.

Didactic messages as samples of other literary genres ameliorate Judeo-Persian poetry. It is in such insertions based both on Judaic and Iranian moral and ethical values of the era that the poet reveals his own social and ethical values. To accomplish this goal, most poets follow the model of Iranian aphoristic literature, such as the *Golestān* and *Bustān* of Sa'di. Nevertheless, the most elaborate example of Judeo-Persian didactic literature is *Ganjnāmeh*, (Book of Treasure), a versified commentary on the *Mishnaic Tracte Abot* (Ethics of the Elders) written by 'Emrāni. This work is closely influenced and dominated by Iranian Persian and Islamic didactic, ethical and mystic values in lyric form.[16]

Variations of the rhetoric arts, mostly in *Khorāsāni* literary style, are seen within the mystic, lyric and didactic passages, as well as the epic accounts representing the secular thematic aspect of Judeo-Persian literature. The use of such rhetoric devices such as harmony of images or congruence of poetic ideas and allusions made by metaphors and similes, as well as antithesis and homophony, in Judeo-Persian verse reflect the level of the sophistication of the poets.

11 حجاب خویش را از پیش بردار   که تا گردی زراه خود خبر دار
حجاب راه تو دام جهانست   نپنداری که اینجا آشیانست

12 ندانستی نباشد دانه بی دام   در افتادی به دام آخر سر انجام

13 به دامت در قفس در بند کردند   به ناکامی ترا خرسند کردند
قفس بشکن که راهی پیش گیری   که گر اندر قفس مانی بمیری

14 خبر داری تو ای طوطی افلاک   چرا کردی گذر در تخته خاک
تو سیمرغی و ایشان مرغ دیگر   نباشد زاغ با طوطی برابر

15 چو عنقا عزلتی بگزیده بودم   زخویش و آشنا بُبریده بودم
چو عنقا اعتزالت گردهد دست   شود درخدمتت خورشید پا بست

16 For partial didactic work on *Ganjnāmeh* in English, see David Yerushalmi. 1995. *The Judeo-Persian Poet 'Emrani and His Book of Treasure, Ganjnameh, a Versified Commentary on the Mishnaic Tracte Abot*, vol. 5. Leiden, New York, and Koln: E.J. Brill.

History of Judeo Persian prose

Historically, Judeo-Persian prose, having its roots in an earlier period, precedes Judeo-Persian verse. In *The Letter of Dandan Uiliq* I, discovered in 1901, and possibly *The Letter of Khotan*, discovered in 2004, are not only the oldest Judeo-Persian prose manuscripts but the oldest New Persian writings. *The Mishnaic Tracte Abot,The letter of Dandan Uiliq* I, concerns trading sheep and the sale of garments of Iranian Jews living in the desert located at the western border of China. *The Letter of Dandan Uliq II* is very similar to *The Letter of Dandan Uiliq I,* in terms of orthography, grammar, archaic words and even use of personal names (Zhang 2010, Irano Judaica Conference, Jerusalem).

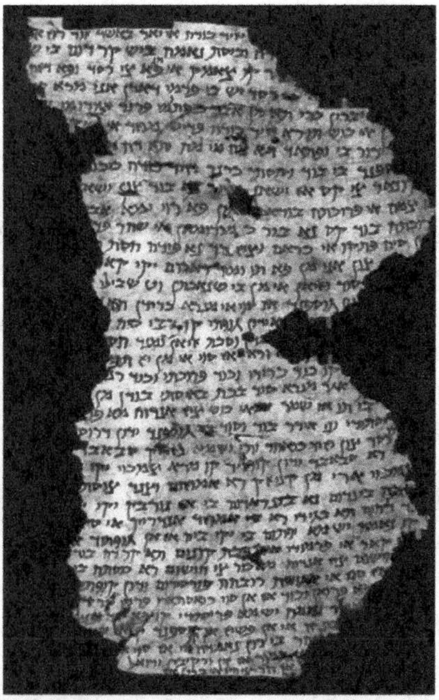

Figure 1.1a The *letter of Dandan Uliq I,* one of the oldest New Persian texts discovered written in Judeo-Persian (circa 750 C.E.)

Source: The Library of British Museum BL17_OR82121661_1

Figure 1.1b The *Letter of Dandan Uliq II.* discovered in (2004 C.E.) by the National Library of China (BH1-19, image reproduced with the kind permission of the National Library of China)[17]

Source: The Library of British Museum BL17_OR82121661_1

17 https://blogs.bl.uk/asian-and-african/2020/06/an-eighth-century-judaeo-persian-letter-from-dandan-uiliq.html; also see: https://commons.wikimedia.org/wiki/Category:Dandan_Uiliq#/media/File:Judeo-Persian_letter_BLI7_OR8212166R1_1.jpg

Except some sporadic documents or items found from the 8th century, the earliest prose writings in hand today are works from the 12th century (Lazard, 48–50). Chronologically, Judeo-Persian prose can be divided into two eras, the pre- and post-Safavid eras.

Translations and commentaries prior to the Safavid era

Works prior to the Safavid era, which coincides with Lazard's periods I & II and Netzer's pre-Mongol era, thematically consisted of exegesis (interpretations) of the Bible, translations and commentaries, translations of exegetic texts in Aramaic and dictionaries. Among this group are: *Commentary on Ezekiel,* 11th century, in the Saint Petersburg library; translation of the *Book of Esther,* in the National Library of Paris (1280 C.E.); Paris manuscript in Perso-Arabic script, translation of *Psalms* (1316 C.E.), transliterated in Perso-Arabic for Giambatista Vecchiettin (1601 C.E.); manuscript of *Pentateuch* at British Museum (1319 C.E.) copied in 1630 C.E. and a four-page commentary (*tafsir*) on Psalms, called as the Fragment from Zefreh, before the 11th century (Netzer 2002). (The originals of some of these documents are lost; thus, the date of the copy is mentioned as well.) Furthermore, some parts of the Babylonian Talmud, as a guideline to Jewish life and traditions, have also been translated and written in Judeo-Persian. Other religious translations include those from books like Proverbs of Solomon; Solomon's Book of Ecclesiastes; the Psalms of David and the Books of Ruth Esther, Isaiah and the Book of Barukh (Netzer 1999a, 89).

Translations and commentaries of the post-Safavid era

Safavid-era commentaries include many Torah translations. Among them are the translation of the Tavus ben Ya'qub ben Yusef, published in 1546 in Istanbul. The Judeo-Persian translation of Tavus was rendered by Thomas Hyde from Hebrew script to Persian script (1657 C.E.). The translation of the Psalms of David (1618) was carried out upon the order of Shah Abbas I and was presented to him in Qazvin. The Afsharid period includes the translation of the Torah, Psalms of David and the New Testament (June 1741), in addition to the translations and commentaries, some parts of the Midrashim, mingled with historical and mythical stories of Iran, that have also been found in Judeo-Persian writings (Netzer 1999a, 89–90).

In addition to *Halakhic* works and books of worship called *siddur*, scholars like Rabbi Yehudah ben 'Elazar have presented *Hovot Yehūdah* (Duties of Judah), in philosophy and theology stories and riddles, dream interpretation, astrology, medicine and dictionaries as the content of other Judeo-Persian writings of that era (Netzer 1999a, 127–133).

Recent findings

In 2010, the Khorasan documents belonging to the pre-Mongol period were discovered in a cave which was home to cattle. Having examined the original manuscripts in London, Prof. Shaul Shaked is convinced that these documents were pages from letters or legal deeds, written for the most part in the Hebrew script and dating back to the medieval period. They also included sections on prayers specifying the order of prayer in the synagogue on various holidays, generally known as *piyyut*. Another portion of these papers consists of personal correspondence, accounts, declarations of debt (*iqrār*) and records of judicial courts. Most of these documents are in Judeo-Persian, in standard Persian or in Arabic (Shaked 2016, IV–XVI).

Masters of Judeo-Persian literature

Judeo-Persian literature is a vast area within the Iranian literary tradition which, due to its Hebrew script, has not yet been fully studied and evaluated. However, in addition to the introduction of some of its major and pioneer contributors, different literary genres and some samples of rhetorical arts used in this branch of Iranian literature are presented. Among the most eminent and prolific ones are:

Shāhīn

Shāhīn was recognized as the first and greatest Judeo-Persian poet. He lived in the 14th century and produced four biblical epics, *Musānāmeh, Ardashīrnāmeh, 'Ezrānāmeh* and *Bereshitnāmeh*. While the Jews of Iran bestowed upon him the venerated title Mowlana Shāhīn, there remains no positive evidence for such an assumption. Shāhīn's first literary piece, *Musānāmeh*, was written in 1327 C.E. and contains about ten thousand verses. This epic piece is a biblically based translation of the last four books of the Pentateuch, which are Exodus, Leviticus, Numbers and Deuteronomy, into Judeo-Persian poetry (Netzer 1996a, 7).

While the literary piece proceeds to describe the episodes of the Israelites from their coming to Egypt, the principal attention as manifested in the title *Musānāmeh* (The Book of Moses) is given to the adventures of the prophet. The high level of poetic and stylistic sophistication as well as the use of vocabulary used in the *Musānāmeh* suggest that Shāhīn intended to compose an epic in imitation of Ferdowsi's *Shāhnāmeh*, the masterpiece of Iranian epic poetry (Netzer 1996a, 7–8)

Ardashīrnāmeh, Shāhīn's second literary work, in contrast to *Musānāmeh*, tells two interrelated stories. The first tells the story of Queen Esther and King Ardashīr (Bahman), and the second describes the complex love story of Shiruyeh, son of Ardashīr and the Chinese Princess Mahzad (Netzer 1996, 8).

As Netzer describes, the six thousand or so couplets paint a spectacular picture of love and revenge, nature and the hunt, battle fields and royal playing fields, the scenes reminiscent of the world described in *Shāhnāmeh* (Netzer 1996a, 8).

Written in five hundred verses, Shāhin's other work, *'Ezrānāmeh*, recounts the life of Cyrus the Great and his encounters with Ezra, Haggai, Zechariah, Mattatya and Mordechai (Netzer 1996a, 8–9). This epic work is considered by scholars to be the continuation of the *Ardashīrnāmeh* since it is also based

Figure 1.2 JTSL Ms. 8270, *Ardashīrnāmeh: 'Ezrānāmeh* folio 4 v

Source: Courtesy of the Library of the Jewish Theological Seminary
Shah Ardashīr is entertained in his harem

on the Book of Ezra and Esther. Furthermore, the particular insertion of information regarding the birth of Cyrus, who according to Shāhīn was born from Esther and Ardashīr, has also led to the reading of the book as an extension of the *Ardashīrnāmeh*.

Shāhīn's fourth and final epic work, *Bereshitnāmeh*, was composed in 1359 and is based on *Sefer Bereshit* (The Book of Genesis). *Bereshitnāmeh* is divided by plot and theme into four parts: from the creation of the world to the binding of Isaac, an epic poem on the subject of Jacob, Joseph and his brothers and the love of Potiphar's wife (*Zoleykhā*) for Joseph (Netzer 1996a, 56–58). While Shāhīn's work is quite faithful to the biblical story, it is not completely divorced from the Islamic narration of the account of Joseph in the Koran (Sura 12). Although *Ardashīrnāmeh* and *Bereshitnāmeh* can be categorized within the epic genre, they can also be considered lyric as well, due to the romantic elements expressed in both accounts (Netzer 1996a, 9).

Figure 1.3 MS. B66.07.1185, Fol. 12 recto 180/054

Source: Courtesy of the Israel Museum, Jerusalem

Moses' mother casts infant Moses into a flaming oven; Miriam, Moses' sister, is putting Moses in a basket on the Nile

'Emrāni

'Emrāni was the second greatest Judeo-Persian poet. Like Shāhīn, he was also given the title Mowlana by the Jews of Iran. His first epic and literary piece, *Fatḥnāmeh,* was written in 1474 as the continuation of Shāhīn's *Musānāmeh* (Netzer 1974a, 208–225). In this respect, *Fatḥnāmeh* begins with the Book of Joshua, followed by those of Ruth and First and Second Samuel. The account continues with a chapter on the conquest of Jerusalem by King David (II Samuel 5:11) and the tributes he received from King Hiram of Tyre (Netzer 1996a, 58–62). Similar to the work of his predecessor, 'Emrāni by his description of glorious battlefields and metalanguage in *Fatḥnāmeh* exhibits an immense amount of influence from Ferdowsi's *Shāhnāmeh.*[18]

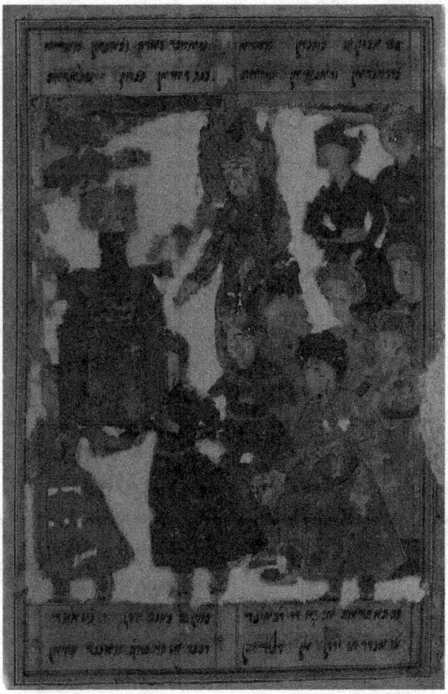

Figure 1.4 MS 964 Fol. 5 verso

Source: Courtesy of Ben Zvi Institute, Jerusalem
Priests carry the Ark of the Covenant over the Jordan River

18 Nahid Pirnazar. 2004. "The Place of the Fifteenth Century Judeo-Persian Religious Epic 'Emrāni's *Fatḥnāmeh* in Iranian Literary Traditions," Doctoral Dissertation. University of California, Los Angeles.
See also Vera Basch Moreen (with Orit Carmeli). 2016. *The Bible As a Judeo-Persian Epic: An Illustrated Manuscript of 'Imrani's* Fath-Nama. Jerusalem: Ben Zvi Institute.

The second epic of 'Emrāni, titled *Ḥanukānāmeh* (1524), describes the resistance of the Maccabees against their Greek oppressors. This piece is also referred to as *Zafarnāmeh*, or "The Book of Victory" (Netzer 1996a, 62). 'Emrāni's apparently last opus, *Ganjnāmeh* (1536), is his five-thousand-couplet poetic adaptation and commentary on the mishnaic, *Pirke Avot*, known as the Wisdom of the Jewish Sages. *Ganjnāmeh*, written in a very eloquent style, is a didactic work reflecting the dual ethical values of the poet, Judaic and Iranian.

Vājebāt va Arkān-e Sizdahgāne-ye Imān-e Isrāel (Thirteen Percepts and Pillars of the Faith of Israel), compiled in 1508, is a shorter didactic work of the poet. As a versified account of Maimonides' (The Thirteen Principles of Faith). This work is composed of seven hundred eighty couplets.

Entekhāb-e Nakhlestān (The Choice of a Palm-Grove), which is aimed at instilling morals and proper conduct in the community and its leaders, is another didactic work of 'Emrāni. It is in this work that 'Emrāni personally associates himself with the geographic locations of Isfahan and Kashan (Netzer 1974, 264).

Sāghināmeh (The Book of the Cupbearer) is among his lyric and non-Jewish compositions with a mystical theme. Although this work of about one hundred ninety couplets is modeled after the *Sāghi-nāmeh* of Hāfez, it is also influenced by the Persian poets Khayyām and Sa'di (Netzer 1996a, 66).

Khāwjeh Bukhara'i

Khāwjeh Bukhara'i was another Judeo-Persian poet of Bukhara, who composed *Dāniālnāmeh* (The Book of Daniel) in 1606 based on the apocryphal book of Daniel and related *Midrashim*.[19] The poetical work consists of more than two thousand couplets, resembling the epic style of the works of Shāhīn and 'Emrāni. *Dāniālnāmeh* contains fascinating descriptions of combats, including when the armies of "Cyrus the Persian and Dariush the Mede" battled against their common enemy, Belshazzar, the last emperor of Babylon (Netzer, 1996b, 12). This is a rare work, with only one complete manuscript left today (Netzer 1996a, 67).

Bābā'i\Ben Loṭf

Bābāi Ben Loṭf is the poet who reported to us about the condition of Iranian Jews during the Safavid era. He wrote his *Ketāb-e Anūsi* (The Book of the

19 Encyclopedia Britannica. S.V. "Midrash": A mode of biblical interpretation prominent in the Talmudic literature (plural Midrashim). The term is also used to refer to a separate body of commentaries on Scripture that use this interpretative mode". https://www.britannica.com/topic/Talmud (accessed June 18, 2020)

Forced Converts) in the years 1656–1662. Although it was written during the reign of Shah 'Abbas II (1642–1667), *Ketāb-e Anūsi* narrates events relevant to Iranian Jewish communities that took place in the reigns of Shah 'Abbas I, Shah Safi I and early Shah 'Abbas II during the years 1613–1660. Aside from Kashan, his birthplace, Bābā'i Ben Loṭf lists nineteen other cities and localities in Iran where Jews lived.

This period was very bitter for the Jews of Iran, and persecutions followed the Jews from city to city. His account corresponds with the reports of Iskandar Beg Torkaman (Monshi),[20] and the Armenian Bishop Arakel of Tabriz, as well as foreigners, especially Pietro della Valle the Italian traveler.[21] Bābā'i Ben Loṭf praises Sheykh Bahā al-Din 'Āmeli for speaking against the forced conversion of Jews as the "People of the Book" and speaks favorably of Shah Safi I (1629–1642), who abrogated the forced conversion of 1625–1629 (Netzer 1996a, 68–70).[22]

Bābā'i Ben Farhād

Bābā'i Ben Farhād, about seventy years later, the grandson or great-grandson of Bābā'i Ben Loṭf, continued the reports of *Ketāb-e Anūsi* in his chronicle named *Ketāb-e Sargozasht-e Kāshān* (The Chronicle of Kashan). This brief chronicle continues with the period of Shah Abbas II, as well as describing the torment of the Jewish population when the Afghans invaded Iran (1722–1730) to overthrow the Safavid dynasty (1502–1736) and the bloody battles that followed (Netzer 1996a, 70).

Mashiaḥ ben Raphael

Mashiaḥ ben Raphael, following Bābāi Ben Farhad, added about eighty lines to *Ketāb-e Anūsi*. His addition, which is basically a repeat of the verses of Bābāi ben Farhad, treats the resistance of the Jews of Kashan against a

20 Eskandar Beig Turkaman, the secretary of the Safavid ruler, Shah 'Abbas I (1581–1629) and the author of *Tarikh-e 'Alamaray-e 'Abbasi*, who recorded the history of Shah 'Abbas I as an eyewitness:
Eskandar Beig Turkaman. 1382/2003. *Tarikh-e 'Alamaray-e 'Abbasi*, 2 volumes, edited by Iraj Afshar (Tehran: Amir Kabir).

21 http://www.iranicaonline.org/articles/della-valle (Accessed May 2014)

22 For further details, see Vera Bach Moreen. 1987. *Iranian Jewry's Hour of Peril and Heroism. A Study of Bābāi Ibn Lotf's Chronicle (1617–1662)*. New York/Jerusalem: The American Academy for Jewish Research, pp. 55–117.
https://commons.wikimedia.org/wiki/Category:Dandan_Uiliq#/media/File:Judeo-Persian_letter_BLI7_OR8212166R1_1.jpg

Figure 1.5 Naqsh-e Jahan Square by Pascal Coste 1 Ver2

Source: ‘Ali Qapu, the residential palace of the Safavids in Naqsh-e Jahan Square, painted in the early 1800s, where, according to Bābā‘i Ben Loṭf and Pietro della Valle, the Jews were forced to convert their religion in front of Shah Abbas I[23]

seven-month forced conversion during the period of Shah Tahmasb II and the rise of Afghans (Netzer 1996a, 70–71).

Aminā: Benjamin ben Mishael

Benjamin ben Mishael, known as Aminā, his *nom de plume*, was born in 1672. Through his work, it can be speculated that he was a spiritual leader in his community because he frequently made references to his popularity and vitality.[24] There are nearly no collections of Judeo-Persian poetry that do not contain several of his poems, showing his high rank. Aminā generally wrote short poems (ten to sixty couplets) on both secular and religious subjects. Some of his works are translations from Hebrew and Arabic. With his poems, Aminā tried to improve the cultural lives of the Jewish community.

In his two poems, *Sargozasht-e Aminā bā Hamsarash* (The Story of Aminā and His Wife), which is a short autobiography, and *Del Sard Shodan az Zan* (The Cooling of the Heart's Passion for Women), Aminā explains his personal married life and the misery he suffered (Netzer, 2003, pp. 37–75).[25]

23 https://fa.wikipedia.org/wiki/%D9%85%DB%8C%D8%AF%D8%A7%D9%86_%D9%86%D9%82%D8%B4_%D8%AC%D9%87%D8%A7%D9%86#/media/%D9%BE%D8%B1%D9%88%D9%86%D8%AF%D9%87:Naqsh-e_Jahan_Square_by_Pascal_Coste_1_Ver2.jpg

24 Amnon Netzer, "The Jewish Poet Amina of Kashan and His Sacred Poems", *Irano Judaica* V, edited by Shaul Shaked and Amnon Netzer. Jerusalem: Ben-Zvi Institute, 2003, p. 73.

25 For English translation of the previous two poems, see Vera Bach Moreen. 2000. *In Queen Ester's Garden*. New Haven/London: Yale University Press, pp. 296–300.

Living and working in Kashan during the late 17th century and the beginning of the 18th century, Aminā enjoyed a rich cultural heritage from both the Muslim and Jewish environments. Some of his approximate contemporaries were poets, writers and scholars such as Moshe Halevy, Bābāi ben Loṭf, Rabbi Yehuda ben El'azar, Bābā'i ben Farhād and others.

Yehudā Ben 'Elāzār

Yehudā Ben Elāzār, the rationalist Jewish philosopher, composed a dissertation entitled *Hovot Yehudah* (Duties of Judah) in Judeo-Persian in 1686. In this unmatched piece of work, Rabbi Yehūda Ben Elāzār strived to analyze the foundations and principles of the Jewish faith in a systematic method based on scientific, rational and philosophical discipline (Netzer 1999, 28).[26]

Rāgheb (Elishā Ben Shmu'el)

Elishā Ben Shmu'el, known as Rāgheb, lived in Samarqand in the 17th century. We know of two of his works:

> *Shāhzādeh va Sūfī* (The Prince and the *Ṣufi*) and *Ḥannukahnāmeh* (*Ḥannuka* Scroll). The first one, as the poet himself acknowledges in his prologue, is based on the Hebrew version of the popular story by the thirteenth century Spanish Jewish scholar Abraham ibn Ḥasdai, "The Prince and the Nazirite". The plot is taken from a well-known Indian tale on the life of Buddha which was translated into Greek and European languages; each version of the story reflecting different beliefs and ideologies as well as motifs modified differently from text to text. The Judeo-Persian version is to encourage a solitary life and purification of the soul in order to distance it from the confines of its bodily "prison" and reunite it with the Godly Source.
>
> (Netzer 1996a, 71–72)

Aharon Ben Māshiah

Aharon Ben Māshiah's *Shofṭimnāmeh* (Book of Judges) was written in 1692. This is a relatively short poem, basically a paraphrase of the first eighteen chapters of the book of Judges. It is usually included in most manuscripts of *Fatḥnāmeh* and is similar in language, style and meter to 'Emrāni's works. In fact, the author mentions 'Emrāni as his teacher and source of inspiration in writing the work (Netzer 1996a, 79).

26 For a brief English review of interpretation of *Hovot Yehūdah: Moreen, In Queen Ester's Garden*, pp. 255–259.

Mordechai ben David has added *Ma'aseh Pilegesh be-Giv'at* (The Tale of the Concubine of Giv 'at), the missing part of the Book of Judges (Netzer 1996a, 83).

Simanṭov Melamed

Simanṭov Melamed was a mystical Judeo-Persian poet, philosopher and author of treatises who lived toward the end of the 18th century. Melamed seems to have been born in Yazd, later relocated to Herat and finally settled in Mashhad, where he became the spiritual leader of the Jewish community. He belonged to a transitional period in Iranian literary history, toward the end of the Isfahani/Hindi literary era and the beginning of the Khorasani literary revival, contemporary with the two masters of the Iranian literary revival, Saba and Neshat. The major work he composed was a philosophical-religious treatise titled *Ḥayat al-Ruḥ* (The Eternity of the Soul), written in prose and verse and heavily based upon the *Ṣufic* ideas of Bahya Ibn Paquda's *Hovot ha-Levavot* (Duties of the Heart).[27]

Melamed's work focuses upon two major mystical and sociological issues. The mystical theme concentrates on a means to reach the final stage of unification with Eternity by discussing various ways in which one can arrive at spiritual perfection. The sociological theme of his text focuses primarily on the deprived minority class of Iranian Jews, whose religious identity is beginning to gradually fade away in the diaspora.

Melamed's prose style is not the same throughout the book, rhyming and decorative in some parts and shallow, using popular words and sentences, in other parts. In terms of verse, he uses ample lines of both Persian and Hebrew verse, some of which are his original work and some of which are from others. Melamed's original pieces of verse are mainly given in the forms of *mathnavi*, *Gazal* (Sonnet) or single lines. Among the later Judeo-Persian authors, he is considered one of the most knowledgeable scholars in Judaism as well as Iranian cultural and religious issues.[28]

27 Bahya Ben Joseph ibn Pakuda: Dayyan and philosopher, he flourished in Saragossa, Spain, in the first half of the 11th century. He was the author of the first Jewish system of ethics, written in Arabic in 1040 under the title "Al Hidayah ila Faraid al-Ḳulub" (Guide to the Duties of the Heart) and translated into Hebrew by Judah ibn Tibbon in the years 1161–80 under the title "Ḥobot ha-Lebabot" (Instruction in the Duties of the Heart); www.jewishencyclopedia.com/articles/2368-bahya-ben-joseph-ibn-pakuda. (accessed August 2, 2017).

28 *Mathnavi*, as a form of Persian poetry, consists of rhyming stitches with unlimited length. *Ghazal:* A ghazal is a poem that is made up like an odd-numbered chain of couplets, where each couplet is an independent poem. The last couplet should refer to the author's name. The rhyming scheme is a---a, b---a, c----a, d-----a, e----a etc. http://www.shadowpoetry.com/resources/wip/ghazal.html (accessed April 2020)

The list of some other Judeo-Persian poets whose names are mentioned here are: Yosef Yehudi of Bukhara, Yehuda ben David of Lar (south of Iran), Shemue'l Pir Ahmad and his son Elisha ' of Kashan, Shahab of Yazd, Aba ben Yosef, Abraham b. Esḥāq, Ebrahim b. Molla Abulkhayr, Elyahou b. Ababa, Aharon Golpayegani, Benyamin b. Elyahou Kashani, Menashe b. Shelemo (Jani Kashmiri), Habib, Hezghia, Haim El 'Azar, Davud Bar Ma'amin, Rahim Hamedani, Refu'a Cohan, Shahedi and Shafighi (whose Jewish identities are not clear), Shahab Yazdi, Gershon Kashani, Mordechai b. Rabbi David, Musa b. Esḥāq, Natan Yazdi, Natan Golpaygani, Hacham Nehoray, Yusof b. Siman Zargani and Yusof b. Aqua.[29] In addition, there is much Judaic folk poetry, in different dialects of Judeo-Persian from different cities. Among them is *Shira-ye Ḥatani* (Wedding Song) in about one hundred eighty lines, a compilation of verses from different cities.

Reverse transliteration of Iranian traditional Persian poetry into Judeo-Persian, like the works of the masters of Iranian poetry, for those illiterate in Perso-Arabic script, is another segment of this vast collection. The same work has been done in prose, including the reverse transliteration of folk stories such as Amir Arsalan, or *Akhlagh-e Moṣṣavar*, the Persian textbook, transliterated by Elyahou Pirnazar. Also, as reported by Jan Rypka, among other non-religious works are the transliterated translation of the *Thousand and One Nights* and Shakespeare's *Comedy of Errors* in Jerusalem (Rypka 1968, 739).

29 For a detailed list of all other poets, see Amnon Netzer. 1996. "Adabiyat-e Yahud-e Iran", part 1, in *Pādyāvand*, edited by Amnon Netzer, vol. 1. Costa Mesa: Mazada Publishers, 1996, pp. 78–84.

2 Thematic contents of Judeo-Persian literature

The thematic content of Judeo-Persian literature may be divided into different categories of verse vs. prose, religious vs. secular and original vs. transliteration.

Literary genres in Judeo-Persian poetry

Gilbert Lazard, divides Judeo-Persian verse, mostly written in the form of *mathnavi*, into two major thematic branches of biblical and apocryphal/midrashic themes.[1]

Biblical epics

Biblical epics are versified accounts of the Five Books of the Pentateuch. The bulk of early period Judeo-Persian works are mainly biblical. The poets who contributed to this genre include:

Shāhin: As the pioneer in this area, Shāhin's works include: *Mūsānameh* (The Book of Moses) compiled c. 1327, recounting four books of scripture; *Ardashīrnāmeh* (The Book of Ardashīr) compiled c. 1316, recounting the story of King Bahman (Ardashīr) and Queen Esther; '*Ezrānāmeh* (The Book of Ezra) covering the reign of Cyrus the Great and the construction of the Second Temple; and *Bereshītnāmeh*, also called *Āfarīneshnāmeh*, recounting the Book of Genesis (Netzer 1996a, 54–58).

'Emrāni: Writing a century after Shāhin, 'Emrāni attempted to complete Shāhin's work by composing *Fatḥnāmeh* (The Book of Conquest) in 1474. Here, he versified the books of Conquest, Ruth and I and II Samuel through the ascension of David to the throne (Netzer 1996a, 58–66).

1 Gilbert Lazard. 1996. "Judeo-Persian Literature", edited by Amnon Netzer, in *Pādyāvand*, vol. 1. Costa Mesa: Mazda Publishers, pp. 45–58.
Mathnavi, as a form of Persian poetry, consists of rhyming stitches with unlimited length.

DOI: 10.4324/9781003031741-3

Aharon ben Māshiaḥ: *Shofīmnāmeh* (The Book of Judges), not covered by 'Emrānī, was versified by Aharon ben Māshiaḥ of Isfahān (1692). The book is missing two chapters of Judges: 19–21 (Netzer 1996a, 76).

Mordechai ben Dāvid: The missing chapter of *Shofīmnāmeh* (Judg. 19–21) that deals with the story of the Levite and his concubine was composed by Mordechai ben Dāvid (Netzer 1996a, 83).

Aminā (Benyanin ben Mishael): *Aqdat Izḥaqh* (Sacrifice of Isaac) (Gen 22: 19), written in 1702, is the versified biblical work of Aminā (Netzer 1996a, 75–76).

Apocryphal and midrashic epics

Many poets have contributed to non-canonical commentary and interpretive works about the Torah. Among the poets who have written in this genre are:

Khwājeh-ye Bukharai: *Dāniālnāmeh* "The Book of Daniel", written in 1606, is an apocryphal account, which covers the story of Daniel. In this work, Khwājeh-ye Bukharai partly covers the history of the Acheamenids, Cyrus and Dariūsh, as well as the downfall of the Babylonian Empire. Later on, Aminā retouched Bukharai's work in 1704 (Netzer 1996a, 66–67).

'Emrāni: As a prolific poet, 'Emrāni contributed in this area as well. *Ḥanūkānāmeh*, "The Book of *Ḥanūkāh*", also known as *Ẓafarnnāmeh*, "The Book of Triumph", was written in 1524 and covers the revolt of the Jews against the Greeks. 'Emrāni's other apocryphal work is *The Story of the Seven Brothers*, which some also call *The Story of Ḥannah and Her Seven Sons*, regarding the Greek occupation of Jerusalem during the Hasmonean period (B.C.E. 140–37). While some scholars like Bacher, Fischel and Lazard consider the author of this account to be Yusof ibn Esḥāq-e Yahūdī, Netzer does approve this assumption (Netzer 1996a, 64).

Rāgheb (Elisha ben Shemuel): In the 17th century, Rāgheb also recounted the story of the Jewish revolt against the Greeks in his own version of *Ḥanūkānāmeh*.

Yusof ibn Esḥāq-e Yahūdī: Yusof ibn Esḥāq-e Yahūdī also has an account regarding the Jewish revolt against the Greeks, titled *Antiākhosnāmeh*, "The Book of Antiochus", written in 1749. According to Netzer, the poet also retouched the aforementioned *The Story of the Seven Brothers*. Yahūdī's version, called *Moṣibatnāmeh* (The Book of Catastrophe), was reportedly completed in 1688 (Netzer 1996a, 72).

Historical narratives

Bābā'ī ben Loṭf and **Bābā'ī ben Farhād:** There are two historically accurate Judeo-Persian poetical works. The first one, *Ketāb-e Anūsī*, "The Book of Forced Converts", by Bābā'ī ben Loṭf, recounts the events of Jews during the reign of Shah 'Abbas I and Shah Ṭahmasb I through the middle of the reign of Shah 'Abbas II, covering the years of 1613 through 1660. The second book, *Ketāb-e Sargozasht-e Kāshān dar bāb-e 'brī va Gū'īmī-ye Sanī*, "The Book of Chronicle of Kashan, Regarding the Second Forced Conversion of the Hebrews", by Bābā'i ben Farhād, mainly recounts the period of Shah 'Abbas II, Shah Thamasb II, the Afghan Invasion and the downfall of the Ṣafavids (c. 1666–1736). The poet also talks about Thamasbgholi, later known as Nader, the founder of the Afsharid dynasty (Netzer 1996a, 68–70).[2]

The events reported by both poets corroborate the memoirs of the contemporary Italian traveler to Iran, Pietro Della Valle and Jean Chardin, the Frenchman living in the court of the Ṣafavids, as well as *Tarik-e 'Ālamāra-ye 'Abbasi*, "Chronicle of Shah 'Abbas the Great", by Eskandar Beg Monshi, his historian, and *The History of Vardapet Arak'el of Tabriz*, written by the contemporary Armenian priest.

Mashiaḥ ben Rafael: later wrote about 80 lines, basically repeating a few incidents already reported by Bābā'i ben Farhād (Netzer 1996a, 70–71).[3]

Romantic lyrics

Shāhīn: In the midst of Shāhin's biblical epics, there are some lyrical and romantic parts, such as the account of *Yūsof va Zolaiykā*, "Joseph and Potiphar's wife", in *Bereshītnāmeh*, as well as the romance of *Shiro & Mahzād*, the son of Shah Bahman, from his prior wife, and the half fairy *Mahzād* in his *Ardashīrnāmeh* (Netzer 1996a, 57, n. 37).[4]

'Emrāni: Romantic lyrical lines in 'Emrāni's works appear mostly as description of the nature and the wedding of David and his second wife Abigale (I Samuel 25: 39–42) in his *Fatḥnāmeh*; the description of Now Ruz, Persian new year and the mystic scenes in his *Sāqīnāmeh*.

2 For further details see Moreen, *Iranian Jewry's Hour of Peril*, pp. 55–117; Pirnazar, *Ketāb-e Anūsi*, transliteration of the book into Perso-Arabic. (forthcoming, Pirnazar, Iran Namag Books series, publisher, Pardis-i Danish).

3 Pirnazar, *Ketāb-e Anūsi*, transliteration of the book into Perso-Arabic. (work in progress).

4 Netzer gives a list of other possible Jewish poets who might have recounted the story of *Yusof va Zoleykhā* in Persian.

Figure 2.1 Fatḥnāmeh (1 Samuel 25: 39–42)

Source: Courtesy of House of Judeo-Persian Manuscripts
Wedding of David and Abigail

Aminā (Benyamin ben Mishael): Aminā's romantic lyrical poems may be found in the forms of sonnets, *mathnavi* and *mostazād*,[5] as he describes women, a walk in the rose garden or a dialogue with his wife (Netzer 1996a 75–76).[6]

Yusof ibn Esḥāgh-e Yahūdī: Yusof ibn Esḥāgh-e Yahūdī composed his lyrical poems in different rhetorical forms of sonnet, eulogy, couplets and *mokhamas*.[7] His longing for his ancestral homeland, Jerusalem, and his desire for redemption are expressed in a short piece, depicting a lover longing for his beloved (Netzer 1996a, 72–73).

Simanṭov Melamed: The lyric insertions in between the ethical, theological and philosophical parts of *Ḥayat-al Ruḥ*, with an embellished rhythmic and rhymed prose, are reminiscent of Sa'dī's *Golestan* or the writings of Khājeh Abd-Allāh Anṣāri, whereas the poetical parts in

5 The literary term *Mathnavi*, applies to rhyming stitches with unlimited length; the term *Mostazad* in Persian rhetorical art is a line with a third stanza, where the third would be repeated in each line.

6 For some translations of Amīna's lyric works, see Moreen, *In Queen Ester's Garden*, pp. 292–330.

7 The literary term *mokhamas* applies to a set of five hemistitches of verse, with the fifth one having a different rhyme.

the form of sonnet, *qaṣīdieh*, couplet and *qaṭ'a* reflect Melamed's literary sophistication.[8]

Mystic lyrics

'Emrāni: The mystic lyrical lines of 'Emrāni in his *Sāqīnāmeh* are considered the best of Judeo-Persian mystic poetry. In his works, 'Emrāni uses mystical terms such as *pardeh* and *hejāb*, "screen and veil", in visiting the image of the *yār* "the beloved", or *rend* "the rogue", *pir-e meykhāneh* or *pir-e moghān*, in describing "the sage", *sama'*, "mystic dance" and other similar terms throughout *Sāqīnāmeh*.[9]

Shāhedi: The *mathnavī* of *Golshan-e Towhīd*, (The Flower Garden of Unity), by someone with the *nom de plume* Shāhedī, is the versified amplification of six hundred lines of Mowlavī's mystic book of *Mathnavī*. Each line of Mowlavī's poem has been expanded by several lines, while the choice of the title might have been modeled after *Golshan-e Rāz*, "The Flower Garden of Secrets", by Sheykh Mad by several line. However, his Jewish identity has not yet been proven (Netzer 1996a, 81).

Rāgheb (Elishah ben Shemuel): Rāgheb from Samarkand composed *Shāhzādeh va Ṣūfī*, "The Prince & the *Ṣufī*", in 1684 as a *mathnavī* of thirty-five chapters. The plot of the story is taken from a tale about the life of Buddha, "Siddhartha Gautama". Later, the account was translated into many European and Middle Eastern languages, including Middle Persian and Hebrew, and dubbed "The Prince and the Nazrite" by Abraham ibn Ḥasdai in 13th-century Spain. As the poet himself acknowledges in his prologue, his work was based on the Hebrew version of the tale (Netzer 1996a, 71).

Simanṭov Melamed: The title of Melamed's work, *Ḥayat-al Ruḥ* (The Eternity of Soul) directly concentrates on a means of reaching the final stage of unification with the divine truth. The text includes a sonnet describing the ṣufis, demonstrating his mystic thoughts as influenced by Islam (Netzer 1996a, 76–77).[10]

8 Also see Moreen, *In Queen Ester's Garden*, p. 298.
The literary term *Qaṣīdeh* refers to an elaborately structured ode of sixty to one hundred lines, maintaining a single *end rhyme* that runs through the entire piece; the same rhyme also occurs at the end of the first hemistich (half-line) of the first verse (Britannica Dictionary); "couplets" or *do beyti*, consist of two successive lines of verse, forming a unit usually marked by rhythmic correspondence, rhyme or the inclusion of a self-contained utterance; "*qaṭ'a*", equivalent to the English "strophe" or "stanza", including either five to six lines of verse about one particular topic or a number of lines of verse forming a separate unit within a poem.

9 For the full text of *Sāqīnāmeh*, see Netzer. 1996. "Adabiyat-e Yahud-e Iran", part 1, pp. 99–106.

10 For the complete work of "Simanṭov Melamed, see Nahid Pirnazar, *Ḥayat al Rūḥ*, transliterated into Perso-Arabic (work in progress).
For samples of his work in English see Moreen, *In Queen Ester's Garden*, pp. 262–265.

Didactic works

'Emrāni: Didactic literature has an important role in both Iranian and Jewish cultures. Thus, it is not surprising that many Judeo-Persian poets always gave advice regardless of the genre they wrote in, embracing both Iranian and Judaic ethics and cultures. An example of this hybrid is found in 'Emrāni's *Ganjnāmeh* (1536), which is a part of *Tracte Abot* (The Wisdom of the Jewish Sages), in the Mishnah. In *Ganjnāmeh*, the short didactic words of Jewish scholars and elders are amplified rhetorically into pages of poetry filled with Iranian ethics, proverbs and legends.

'Emrāni's other didactic work is *Vājebāt va Arkān-e Sizdahgāneh-ye Imān-e Isrāel* (Thirteen Percepts and Pillars of the Faith of Israel) compiled in 1508. This work is based on the Thirteen Principles of the Faith, revised by Maimonides (b. 1135–1204).

In a more personal text, *Entekhā b-e Nakhlestān* (Choice of a Palm Grove), 'Emrāni gives religious, moral, and practical advice to the members and leaders of his community and family.[11]

Simanṭov Melamed: *Ḥayat al Rūḥ* is a compilation of ethical speeches combined with philosophical explanations by Judaic scholars and verses of poetry or prose in the manner of Iranian literary masters. The ethical, theological and philosophical parts of the book, as embellished rhythmic, rhymed prose, remind us of the *Golestan* of Sa'di or the writings of Khājeh Abd-Allāh Anṣāri, while the verse parts in the form of sonnets, *qaṣideh*, couplets and *qaṭ'a* reflect his Iranian literary sophistication (Netzer 1996a, 76–77).[12]

Yehūdā ben Davīd: Yehūdā ben Davīd, also known as Yehūdā Lāri or Yehūdā Shirazi, is another contributor to the genre of ethics with his compilation *Makhzan al-Pand* (The Treasure of the House of Exhortation). The title and the content were likely modeled after the *Makhzan al-Asrār* of 'Aṭṭar-e Neyshaburi (d. 1220). Proverbs of Solomon is another didactic work of the poet (Netzer, 1996a, 77–78).[13]

11 For an introduction to 'Emrāni's works and partial translation of 'Emrāni's *Ganjnāmeh* in English, check David Yerushalmi. 1995. *The Judeo-Persian Poet 'Emrani.*

12 Nahid Pirnazar, "Simanṭov Melamed, the Judeo Persian Writer and Poet", conference at Association for Iranian Studies, Vienna, 2016.

13 For English translation of some of Melamed's works, see Moreen, *In Queen Ester's Garden*, pp. 176–183.

Panegyric works

Panegyric poetry, usually used for praising the monarchs and people of authority, as a by-product of the sociocultural and economic status of the Jews, has been very scarce in Judeo-Persian poetry. As a minority, Jews were hardly given positions in the court, nor did they have contact with high-ranking officials. However, few samples of panegyric work that praised the royalty may be found in Shāhin's *Ardashīrnāmeh*, in which he praises Solṭan Abū Sa'īd Khān (d. 1336). Praise of Shah Ashraf (d. 1730) may also be found in Aminā's works (Netzer 1973, 113–114).[14] Praising the Almighty, the prophet Moses and other religious figures such as Aaron is frequent in most Judeo-Persian collections (Netzer 1973, 111–113).[15]

Religious prayer

Prayers, called *monjājāt*, are another segment of Judeo-Persian literary works, usually found in most Judeo-Persian collections. This type of poetry is often seen at the introduction of a poetic collection such as in the introduction of Aharon Ben Māshiaḥ in his *Shofṭimnāmeh*. The other occasions when prayers were used was at the time of catastrophes, such as the longing for redemption by Yousof ben Esḥāq Yahūdi, saying:

In waiting for salvation, if my patience and tolerance are gone,
I will not worry as you are my hope.[16]

Satirical poetry

Satirical works in Judeo-Persian poetry are rare but may be found hidden in the content of other accounts, such as in 'Emrāni's *Entekhāb-e Nakhlestān*, when the poet is complaining about the ill-natured people of Isfahan who finally forced him leave for Kashan. In this respect he says:

If they saw my shadow on the wall,
They would scratch it out with their nails[17]

Aminā was also no stranger to satire, as evidenced when he wrote about his wife in two poems, *Sargozasht-e Aminā bā Hamsarash* (The Story of Aminā and His Wife) a short autobiography, and *Del Sard Shodan az Zan*,

14 For English translation, see Moreen, *In Queen Ester's Garden*, pp. 289.

15 For English translation of other such poems, see Moreen, *In Queen Ester's Garden*, pp. 270–280.

16 Netzer, "Adabiyat-e Yahud-e Iran. pt. 1, 1996a, p. 73:

گنولا برد اگر صبر و قرارم امیدم چون تویی هیچ غم ندارم

17 Yerushalmi, *The Judeo-Persian Poet 'Emrani*, pp. 26–27.

اگر نقشم بدیدندی به دیوار بکردندی ز ناخن ناپدیدار

"The Cooling of the Heart's Passion for Women". In both poems, Aminā relays the misery of married life in a satirical manner telling his son:

O my heart, light of my soul, listen to me!
If you do not ever wish to be
Buried without a shroud,
Don't tie your heart to a woman[18]

Folklore poetry

The most popular Iranian Jewish folk song is the *Shirā-ye Hātānī*, "The Wedding Song", which is about one hundred fifty couplets. Every city and dialect has added its own personalized lines, and it is sung not only at weddings but most happy Jewish celebrations (Netzer 1996a, 107–114).

Translations and transliterations of secular Iranian poetry

A large portion of Judeo-Persian works in verse are either translations or amplifications of the works of the masters of Persian poetry like Sa'di, Hafez, Khayyām, Jāmi, Mowlavi, Neẓāmī, Bābā Ṭaher-e Oryān and many others (Netzer, 1996a, 97–98).

18 Netzer, 2003, 37–75.
For full English translation, see Moreen, *In Queen Ester's Garden*, pp. 298–300.
ای دل بیا بشنو زمن   خواهی نمیری بی کفن   هرگز نبندی دل به زن
بشنو زمن جان پدر   باشد لبش گر نیشکر   هرگز نبندی دل به زن ....

3 Thematic contents of Judeo-Persian prose

Translations and commentaries on the Hebrew Bible

Early Judeo-Persian prose consists mostly of commentaries and translations of Aramaic texts called *targum*, "translation". The term refers to the explanation of the Hebrew Scripture in Western Aramaic for those Jews who at the time had partially or completely ceased to understand the language of the Scripture. The Judeo-Persian translations of *targum* include a large bulk of religious texts and commentaries on the Books of Esther and Ezekiel as well as the original copies of some of the translations of the Torah and Apocrypha (Netzer 1999a, 88–89). Nevertheless, the very first translation of the Scripture into Perso-Arabic is the first six chapters of the Book of Genesis by Abhi Chand, the Hindu disciple of **Sa'īd** Sarmad Kashi, recorded in the book *Dabestan al-Mazaheb*, "The School of Manners".[19]

Recent Judeo-Persian and Perso-Arabic translations, mostly done by the British and Foreign Bible Society of London (1895–1907), conclude the biblical Judeo-Persian writings (Netzer 1999a, 90–91).

Halakhic works

Halakhic works dealing with Jewish laws and legal matters mostly include medieval legal works of Iranian Jews based on the legal guidance of Maimonides' *Mishneh Torah* (1135–1204) and Josef Caro's *Shulhan Arukh* (1488–1575). The legal matters include slaughter, burial, shrouding, mourning, wedding, marriage, circumcision and divorce rituals and issues (Netzer 1999a, 125–126).

19 Walter J. Fischel. 1948–49. "Jews and Judaism at the Court of the Moghul Emperors in Medieval India", *Proceedings of the American Academy for Jewish Research*, vol. 18. New York: Ktav Publishing House, pp. 137–177.

DOI: 10.4324/9781003031741-4

Among the scholars contributing to *Halakhic* works and books of worship, Rabbi Yehuda Ben 'Elāzār's *Hovot Yehūdah* (Duties of Judah), deals with the fundamental principles of Jewish belief and philosophy. These principles are presented systematically, from both a traditional religious-legal and a philosophical—or, as the author puts it, rational—perspective. The four main parts of the book correspond to the four principles of Jewish faith asserted by Yehudā Ben Elāzār, as opposed to the thirteen principles of Maimonides (Netzer 1995, i).

Liturgical works: siddurs

Most siddurs (prayer books), found in Nathan Adler's visit to Tehran and Bukhara (1896–1897) were later transferred to the Jewish Theological Seminary in New York. Among such books are those on *Seliḥot* "special prayer for forgiveness", which are read from the beginning of the month of Elul, the last month of the Jewish year, until the day of Yom Kippur "the Day of Atonement" (Netzer 1999a, 122–123).

Works on philosophy, theology and mysticism

The prominent prose works in these areas are the *Hovot Yehūdah* (Duties of Judah). by Rabbi Yehūdah ben 'Elāzār on philosophy and theology and *Ḥayat al Rūḥ* by Simanṭov Melamed on mysticism and the manner of unification with God (Netzer 1999a, 127–132).

Stories and riddles

Works on stories and riddles, based on Jewish and Iranian, as well as Islamic, sources, were first written in the 14th century. These texts are mostly didactic, derived from *midrashim* "sermons", mingled with historical and mythical stories of Iran (Netzer 1999a, 132–133).

Dream interpretation and astrology

Original works on dream interpretation and astrology have been found as early as the 10th century and today mostly have an anthropological importance (Netzer 1999a, 133).

Judeo-Persian dictionaries

Among the list of Judeo-Persian dictionaries, the most important one—from Hebrew to Persian—is *Sefer ha-Meliṣah* from the 14th century, which defines biblical, Talmudic and *midrashic* vocabulary. It also contains words in the Khwārazm dialect.

Another dictionary, titled *Argon*, was compiled by Musā ben Hārun ben She'rit in Shirvān in 1459. So far, one incomplete copy of this dictionary has been located (Netzer 1999a, 133–134).

Medical works

Medical books were probably brought from Greece during the Sassanid period, and their principles were taught at the Jundi Shapour Medical School. Also, Indian and Chinese medicine had an impact on Irano-Islamic medicine. Some of such medical books written in Persian or Arabic were transliterated or translated into Judeo-Persian. The earliest such books are *Al-Kāfī* in the 11th century and *Zak`hīreh-ye Khwārazmshāhī* on the early 12th century based on the *Canon* of Avicenna (Netzer 1999a, 135–136).

Journalism and secular publications

Shalom magazine, published before the Balfour declaration and the rise of Zionism in Iran, basically intended to raise the level of intellectual knowledge of Iranian Jews, report on the conditions and problems of the Jewish community and finally be the means of communication between Iranian Jews from different cities (Levy 1999, 518; Netzer 1996a, 299–309; Jaleh Pirnazar 2000, 15–17).

Ha-Ge'ula (the redemption) was the official publication of the Zionist Association and politically had a submissive attitude, with no intention of interference in the matters of the state. It included translations from foreign magazines, instruction in Hebrew language, translations of modern Jewish literature and biblical quotations to strengthen the messianic character of Persian Jewry's conception of Zionism (Levy 1999, 530; Jaleh Pirnazar 2000, 18–19).

Ha Haim (Life), established and edited by Shemuel Haim, was a weekly publication that expressed the editor's aspirations for Iranian Jews as a member of the Iranian nation. It was set up as a means of communication with the Jewish community on a political basis (Levy 1999, 530; Netzer Encyclopaedia Iranica S.V. "Shemuel Haim"; Jaleh Pirnazar, 2000, 19–20).

In addition to the previous writings and publications, the minutes of the Zionist Organization of Iran from 1917 to 1923 have recently been found in Judeo-Persian script, too. The writing of these minutes by highly educated Iranian Jews, who were certainly literate in Perso-Arabic, aside from convenience, is another indication of the sense of privacy needed by Iranian Jews to document their writings.

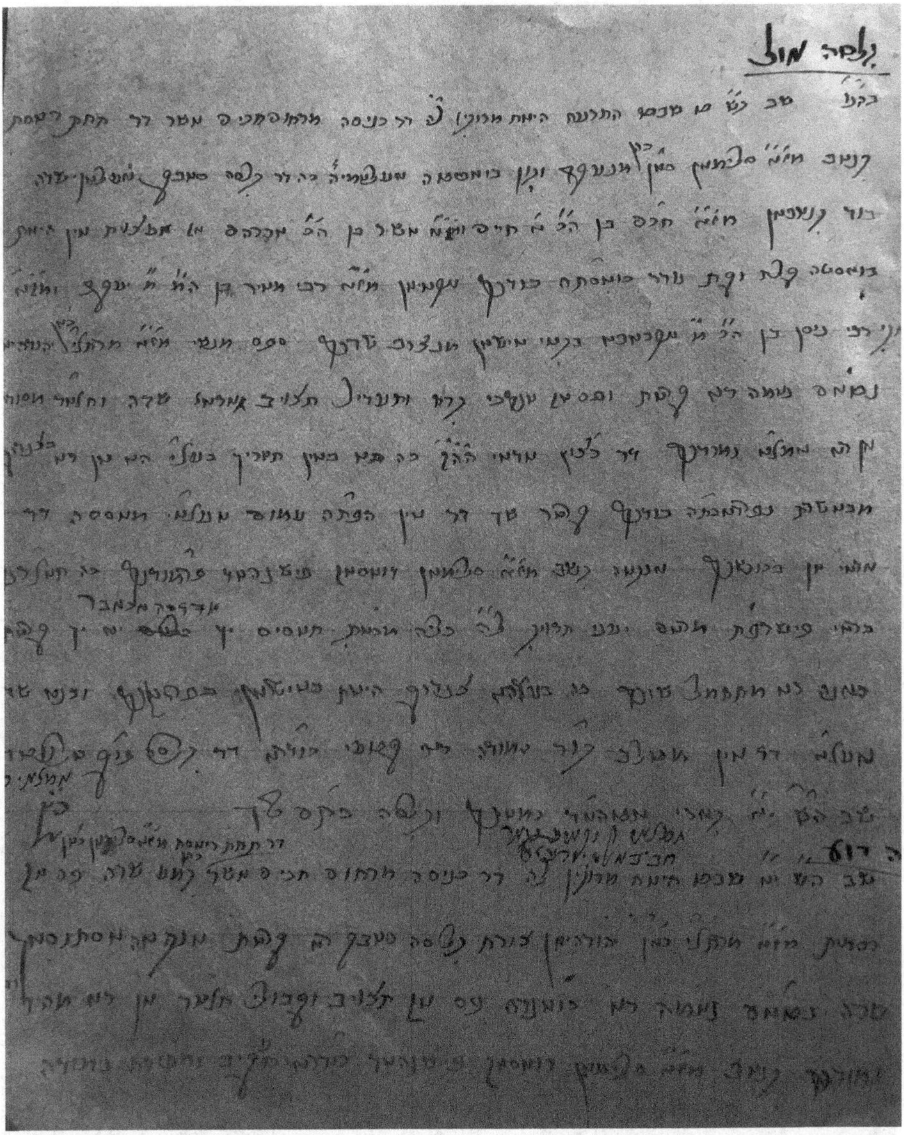

Figure 3.1 Tehran Zionist's minutes book. Samples of handwritten minutes of the Zionist Organization

Source: Courtesy of Habib Levy Cultural Foundation

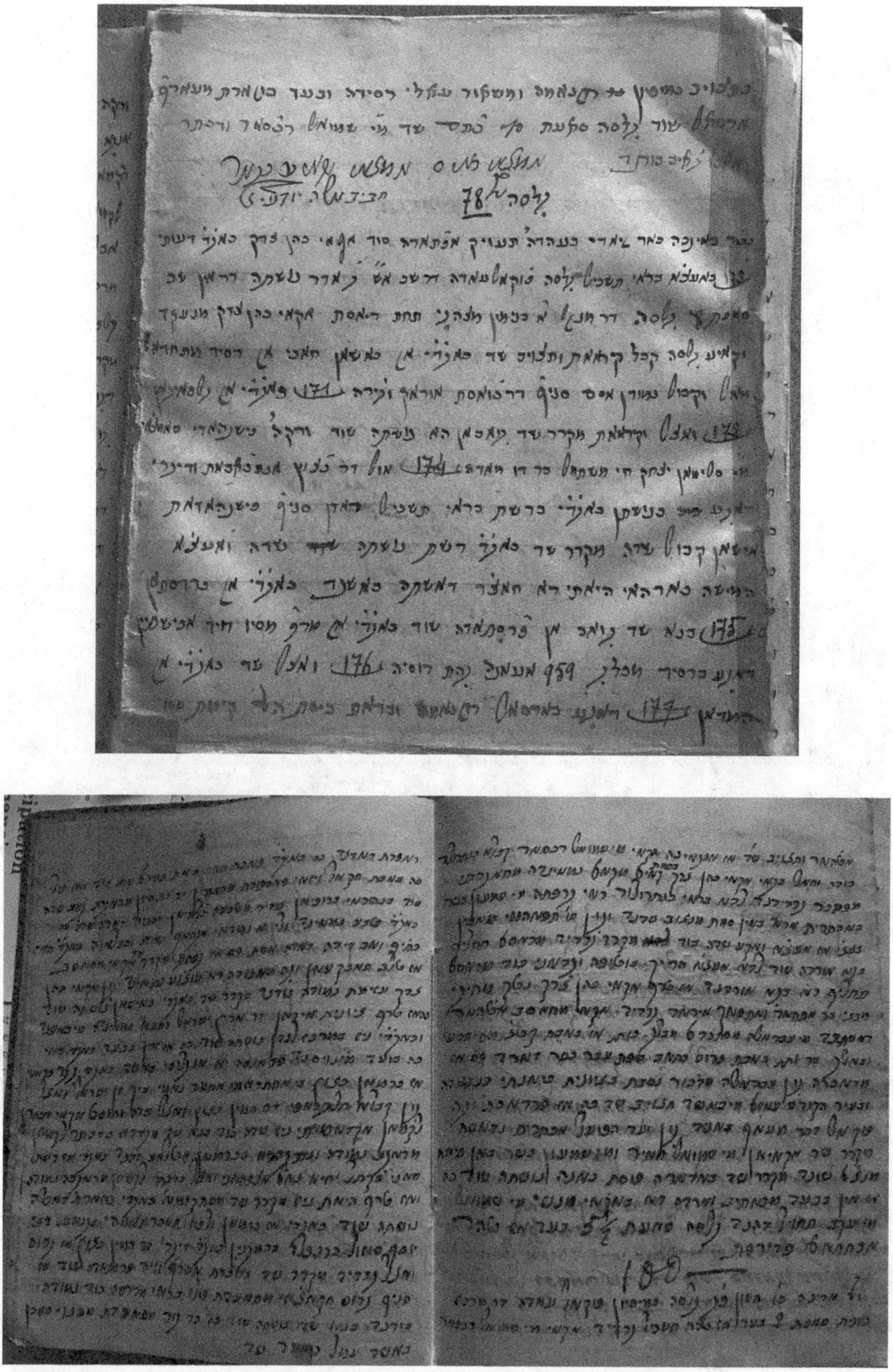

Figure 3.1 (Continued)

Conclusion

Life in the diaspora for twenty-seven centuries and more than ten centuries away from the center of Judaism had caused a lack of familiarity with the Hebrew language and acquaintance with their Judaic legacy for Iranian Jews. Except for those literate in Hebrew and biblical writings, reading about their religious heritage in Judeo-Persian certainly played an important role in the preservation of the lay people's Jewish identity.

Recent discoveries of Judeo-Persian writings in Afghanistan, Geniza or those previously found outside of the contemporary borders of Iran depict the vast demographic spread of Iranian Jews within the greater Iranian land mass. Through their intellectual and literary contributions, Judeo-Persian authors have in time submitted a legitimate claim to inclusion in the development of Iranian heritage. In the meantime, by writing their Judaic beliefs and traditions in Judeo-Persian, they have also maintained their religious identity, which otherwise would have faded.

As a result of the adoption of the Iranian Constitution (1906), a new page was turned, and the religious minorities of Iran found a new sociocultural life. Now recognized as Iranian citizens, Jews were no longer confined to Jewish quarters and schools. Civil rights and a national system of education offered Jews a command of Perso-Arabic script. This new freedom empowered their Iranian national identity and influenced many to put the use of Judeo-Persian aside. By the second half of the 20th century, the array of Judeo-Persian works was left untouched on the shelves of world libraries, giving Iranian Jews a chance to share their cultural contributions with the rest of the Iranians in Perso-Arabic script.

Regardless of period and style, Judeo-Persian literature resonates with the voice of talented Iranian Jews who feel great attachment to their Iranian culture and language as well as to their Judaic heritage. The study of Judeo-Persian literature contributes to the rich literary tradition of Iranian mosaic culture, as well as to the people whose intellectual life has not been recorded due to script, religious and socioeconomic barriers. Also, as a Judaic literary contribution, the work is a representation of the literary activity of Middle Eastern Jews not so well recognized in Judaic global literature.

Part II

Samples of Judeo-Persian writings

Judeo-Persian transliteration chart

Consonant chart

Table 1.1 Consonant chart

Standard Hebrew print	*Selected JP script**	*Selected JP print*	*Standard Persian print*	*Phonetic chart ***
א	א	א	أ / آ	**A**
ב/בּ	ב	ב	ب	**B**
פ / ף	פ / ף	פ / ף	پ	**P**
ת	ת / ט	ת / ט	ت	**T**
	ת' / ס	ת'	ث	**S**
	גִ	גִ	ج	**J**
	גֶ / צֶ / ץֶ	גֶ / צֶ / ץֶ	چ	**Ch**
ח	ח	ח	ح	**Ḥ**
	כ' / ך'	כ' / ך'	خ	**Kh**
ד	ד	ד	د	**D**
	ד'	ד'	ذ	**Z**
ר	ר	ר	ر	**R**
ז	ז	ז	ز	**Z**
	ז'	ז'	ژ	**Zh**
ס / ש'	ס	ס	س	**S**
ש'	ש	ש	ش	**Sh**
/צ / ץ	ס/צ / ץ	ס/צ / ץ	ص	**Ṣ**
	צ' / ץ'	צ' / ץ'	ض	**Ż**
ט	ט / ת	ט / ת	ط	**Ṭ**
	ט' / ז	ט' / ז	ظ	**ẓ**
ע	ע	ע	ع	**‘**
	ג'	ג'	غ	**Gh**
פ / ף	פ' / ף'	פ' / ף'	ف	**F**
ק	ק	ק	ق	**Q**
כ / ך	כ / ך'	כ / ך	ک	**K**

(*Continued*)

DOI: 10.4324/9781003031741-6

Table 1.1 (Continued)

Standard Hebrew print	*Selected JP script**	*Selected JP print*	*Standard Persian print*	*Phonetic chart ***
ג	ג	ג	گ	G
ל	ל	ל	ل	L
מ / ם	מ / ם	מ / ם	م	M
נ / ן	נ / ן	נ / ן	ن	N
ו	ו / ו'	ו / ו'	و	V/U
ה	ה	ה	ه	H
	י / י'	י	ی	Y

Vowel chart

Table 1.2 Vowel chart

א	א	א	آ / ا	Ā/A
י	י	י	ی /ایی	Ī/I
ו	ו /'-	ו/'-	ُ/ او	Ū/O
וו	וו	וו	َو	AW/Ow
יי	יי	יי	َی / ِی /	Ay/Ey

* Judeo-Persian script is not standardized, and different scribes have used many Hebrew print alphabet and some Rashi characters in their copies of the manuscripts as they individually determined.

**The *International Journal of Middle Eastern Studies* chart.

Rashi script

Rashi script, based on 15th-century Sephardic semi-cursive handwriting, is named after Rashi, the author of rabbinic commentary on the Hebrew Bible and Talmud. It is customarily used for printing his commentaries. As a Sephardic origin script, it has been used as a model for printed Judeo-Spanish and other Sephardic Jewish writings, including some Judeo-Persian manuscripts.

Table 1.3 Rashi alphabet chart

ט = ט	ח = ח	ז = ז	ו = ו	ה = ה	ד = ד	ג = ג	ב = ב	א = א
ס = ס	ן = ן	נ = נ	ם = ם	מ = מ	ל = ל	ך = ך	כ = כ	י = י
ת = ת	ש = ש	ר = ר	ק = ק	ץ = ץ	צ = צ	ף = ף	פ = פ	ע = ע

Transliteration Methodology

Transliterated samples used in this collection are taken from the following sources:[1]

Amnon Netzer, "Adabiyat-e Yahud-e Iran", in *Pādyāvand.*
Amnon Netzer, *Montakhab-e Ashār-e Fārsi āz Āsār-e Yahūdīāyān-e Irān.*
Aharon Ben Mashiaḥ Isfahani, *Shofṭimnāmeh,* ms. BZI 964.
Bābā'i Lotf, *Ketāb-e Anūsi,* ms. BZI 917.
'Emrāni, *Fatḥnāmeh,* ms. BZI 964.
'Emrāni, *Ḥanukāhnāmeh,* ms. BZI 2075.
Simanṭov Melamed, *Ḥayat al-Ruḥ ms.* BZI 5760 8 o.
Irano-Judaica, vol. 1. Jerusalem: Ben Zvi Institute. pp. 204–264.
Four Doors decorated with illustrations and poetic writings, displayed at the Light and Shadow Conference, Tel Aviv University, 2010, UCLA 2012.

All transliterated texts have been revised and written in print form by the editor. Except for a few cases, no suggestion is given regarding the non-paralleled rhymes or rhythmic discrepancies.

In the case of orthographic or grammatical inconsistencies, since JP texts are not written in a standardized format, some corrections have been made to facilitate the reading for non–Hebrew literate readers.

Certain vowels and punctuation marks are added to the Perso-Arabic transliterated version for clarity.

With the exception of a few Arabic words and titles, transliterations are made according to the Persian pronunciation and spelling suggested by the *International Journal of Middle Eastern Studies,* with some modificaitions.

Sometimes in rhyming the lines, we find the vowels /**ā**/ and /**ū**/ used as parallels, such as:

/**ā**/ in /*penhān*/ (پنهان) rhymed with /**ū**/ in /*malūn*/(ملعون); *yahudān* (یهودان) with *birūn* (بیرون).

Sometimes for rhythmic reasons, long vowels are replaced with short vowels, such as:

/**ū**/ in /*būdan*/ (بودن)pronounced or written with /**o**/ in /b**o**dan/ (بُدن), or the one vowel is dropped, as in the case of: *ke*-ey (که ای) pronounced and written as /kay/ (کِی).

1 Amnon Netzer. 1973. *Montakhab-e Ashār-e Fārsi āz Āsār-e Yahūdīāyān-e Irān* [Selected Persian Poetry, Heritage of the Jews of Iran]. Edited by Amnon Netzer. Tehran: Farhang-e Iran Zamin. Amnon Netzer. 1996a. "Adabiyat-e Yahud-e Iran," [Persian Literature], in *Pādyāvand,* edited by Amnon Netzer, vols. 1 and 3. Costa Mesa: Mazada Publishers.

Biblical Epic Poetry

פדשאהי כרדן כיי ארדשיר
پادشاهی کردن کی‌اردشیر
The Reign of King Ardashīr[1]

1. סר זד ג̣ו קמר ז ב'רג̇ מאהי   דאד או בה ג̇האן צלאי שאהי
2. ג̣ון שיר ש'ד ארדשיר בר תכ'ת   אן כ"סרוו מהוש ג̇ואן בכ'ת
3. ג̣ון סרו' סהי נשסת בר גאה   בר תכ'ת כיאן זנוו שד או שאה
4. בר סר בנהאד תאג̇ גשתאסב   אראסתה כרד גאה להראסב
5. סר דר בר או סראן נהאדנד   שאדאן בר תכ'תש איסתאדנד
6. אז לעל ו ד'רש נת'אר כרדנד   תעצ'ים ו'יי אשכאר כרדנד
7. כרדנד המה כ'לק אפ'רינש   בר מסנד ו גאה ו בר נגינש
8. בהמן בה ה'נרו'ראן בפ'רמוד   שאהי ג̣ו בה מן בדאד מעבוד
9. אנדר פיי עדל ו דאד באשם   דר דידה צ"לם כ'אר באשם

۱. سر زد چو قمر ز برج ماهی   داد او به جهان صلای شاهی

1 From the house of Pisces he emerged as a victor,
To the world he declared his royal proclamation.

۲. چون شیر شد اردشیر بر تخت   آن خسرو مهوش جوان بخت

2 Like a lion, Ardashīr ascended the throne,
That moon-faced monarch with a bright fortune.

۳. چون سرو سهی نشست بر گاه   بر تخت کیان ز نو شد او شاه

3 Like a towering cypress, he sat on the throne,
On that royal seat, his kingship began anew.

۴. بر سر بنهاد تاج گشتاسب   آراسته کرد گاه لهراسب

4 Crowning himself with the crown of Goshtasb,
He adorned the seat of Lohrasp.

۵. سر در بر او سران نهادند   شادان بر تختش ایستادند

5 By his throne bowing to him,
Joyfully, stood the noblemen.

۶. از لعل و دُرش نثار کردند   تعظیم وی آشکا ر کردند

6 They showered him with rubies and pearls,
Ceremoniously paying their respects.

۷. کردند همه خلق آفرینش   بر مسند و گاه و بر نگینش

7 All men then praised him,
For his throne and the seal of his kingship.

1 Netzer, *Montakhab*, p. 132: *Ardashīrnameh* by Shāhīn.

۸. بهمن به هنروان بفرمود   شاهی چو بمن بداد معبود

8 Bahman proclaimed, addressing the nobles,
"Now that the Kingdom has been bestowed on me,"

۹. اندر پیِ‌عدل و داد باشم   در دیدهٔ ظلم خار باشم

9 "I shall pursue the path of justice and fairness,
Shall be a thorn in the eyes of the unjust.

אגאהי יאפ'תן שאה בהמן אז ופ'את רסתם זאל
آگاهی یافتن شاه بهمن از وفات رستم زال
King Bahman Learns of the Death of Rostam, son of Zal[2]

1. דריאב שהא כה ר'סתם זאל   אן צאחב רכ'ש ו תיג' וכופאל
2. דרגָהשג'אדבהדרגהאפ'תאד   פ'אני שד ו בא זו'ארה גָאן דאד
3. דרגאהש'דןגָומילבפרדאכ'ת   תירי ז כמאן גָאגָי אנדאכ'ת
4. בר נאף' שג'אד בה דרגה דון   רוח אז בר או ברפ'ת בירון
5. גָון קאתל כ'ויש רא פ'נא כרד   או הם בש'ד ו גָהאן רהא כרד
6. בהמן גָו שניד ר'סתם ג'רד   בא הר דו בראדראן גָנאן מ'רד
7. בר ר'סתם זאבלי בסי זאר   בגריסת ז גָוור גָרד' ג'דאר
8. ר'אנגה זפדר גָו אמדש יאד   בר כשתן אן ילאן בשד שאד

۱. دریاب شها که رستم زال   آن صاحبِ رخش و تیغ و کوپال

1 Be informed, Majesty, that Rostam, son of Zal,
The horseman who rode the Rakhsh holding his sword.[3]

۲. در چاهِ‌شغاد به‌در گه افتاد   فانی شد و با زواره جان داد

2 Fell in the end into Sheghad's well,
Perished and lost his life along with Zavareh.

۳. در گاهِ شدن چو میل بپرداخت   تیری ز کمانِ چاچی انداخت

3 At the time of action he felt so inclined,
To shoot an arrow from his *chachi* bow.

۴. بر نافِ شغاد به در گه دون   روح از بر او برفت بیرون

4 Into the belly of the mischievous Sheghad,
Causing his soul to leave his body.

۵. چون قاتل خویش را فنا کرد   او هم بشد و جهان رها کرد

5 Having slain his killer,
He too departed and left this world.

۶. بهمن چو شنید رستم گُرد   با هر دو برادران چنان مُرد

6 When Bahman heard that the hero Rostam,
Had perished with both his brothers in that manner.

2 Netzer, *Montakhab*, p. 134-135: *Ardashīrnameh* by Shāhīn.
3 Rakhsh is the name of Rostam's horse.

۷. بر رستم زابلی بسی زار   بگریست ز جور چرخ غدار

7 He cried with great agony for Rostam of Zabol,
Lamenting the cruel vicissitudes of fate.

۸. وانگه ز پدر چو آمدش یاد   بر کشتن آن یلان بشد شاد

8 But when he remembered his father,
He felt joy in the death of those stout men.

ג̇מע כרדן זלייכ'א כ'אתונאן מצר רא ו יוסף' עליה אלסלאם באישאן נמודן
جمع کردن زلیخا خاتونان مصر را و یوسف علیه السلام بایشان نمودن
Zoleikha Gathers the Egyptian Ladies to See Joseph[4]

1. זלייכ'א כרד רוזי מיזבאני   נהאד או תאזה בזם כ'סרו'אני
2. זנאן מהתראן שהר רא כ'אנד   בכ'לו'תכ'אנהשאן או שאד בנשאנד
3. זמאני עשרת ו שאדי בכרדנד   פ'ראו'אן נעמת שאהאנה כ'ורדנד
4. בה ו'צל הם זמאני שאד בודנד   ערוסאן ג̇מלה בי דאמאד בודנד
5. זלייכ'א שאן בנ'אזש האי בסאר   בכרדי הר זמאן זאן לפ'ט' ד'ר באר
6. נהאד אנדר זמאן אן שוך' פ'ר פ'ן   ת'רנג̇ וכארד דר דסת הר זן
7. בגפ'תא כארד ברדאריד אז ג̇א   כ''ריד הר יך תרנג̇ כ'יש תנהא
8. זלייכ'א דאשת יוסף' רא נהפ'תה   דרון כ'אנה המג̇ו ג'ל שכפ'תה
9. זני נאגה דר אן כ'אנה בגשאד   בש'ד יוסף' רו'אן ג̇ון סרו' אזאד
10. ש'עאע ח'סן או דר מג̇לס אפ'תאד   זבזם דלבראן ברכ'אסת פ'ריאד
11. זשוק ח'סן או מדהוש גשתנד   המה סרגשתה וביהוש גשתנד
12. נשאן זנדגי דר כ'וד נדידנד   ת'רנג̇ ודסת רא דר הם ברידנד
13. ג̇באן מ'סתג'רק אן חור גשתנד   כה אז הסתי כוד אנדר גד'שתנד
14. זזכ'ם אן תרנג̇ ודסת פ'ר כ'ון   בגשתאן דלבראן רא ג̇אמה פ'ר כ'ון
15. בגפ'תנד חאשא ללאה אין בשר ניסת   ג̇מאלש ג'ז פ''רוג' מאה וכ'ור ניסת
16. פ'רשתה אסת או ויא חור בהשת אסת   נהאלש רא בני אדם נכשת אסת

۱. زلیخا کرد روزی میزبانی   نهاد او تازه بزم خسروانی

1 One day, as hostess Zoleikha,
Arranged a novel royal reception.

۲. زنان مهتران شهر را خواند   بخلوت خانه شان، او شاد بنشاند

2 She invited all the noble women in town,
And seated them happily in her private chamber.

۳. زمانی عشرت و شادی بکردند   فراوان نعمت شاهانه خوردند

3 They spent some time in joy and happiness,
And enjoyed the lavish royal feast.

4 Netzer, *Montakhab*, pp. 77–78: *Breshitnameh* (Book of Genesis) by Shāhīn.

۴. به وصل هم زمانی شاد بودند   عروسان جمله بی داماد بودند

4 All the maidens enjoyed each other's company,
Not having their menfolk around.

۵. زلیخاشان نوازش های بسیار   بکردی هر زمان زان لفظ دُرّ بار

5 Zuleika treated them most kindly.
Showered upon them words of praise.

۶. نهاد اندر زمان آن شوخ پرفن   ترنج و کارد در دست هر زن

6 At the same time, the artful hostess placed,
An orange and a knife in each of their plates.

۷. بگفتا کارد بردارید از جا   خورید هر یک ترنج خویش تنها

7 And asked them to pick up the knives,
And peel and eat their oranges.

۸. زلیخا داشت یوسف را نهفته   درون خانه همچو گل شکفته

8 Having hidden Joseph somewhere within the chamber,
Like a blooming rose but hidden from view.

۹. زنی نا گه در آن خانه بگشاد   بشد یوسف روان چون سرو آزاد

9 She then ordered the door open,
And Joseph, like a towering cypress, walked in.

۱۰. شعاع حسن او در مجلس افتاد   ز بزم دلبران بر خاست فریاد

10 A ray of his beauty shone upon the assembly,
And made the beautiful ladies scream in awe.

۱۱. ز شوق حسن اومدهوش گشتند   همه سر گشته و بیهوش گشتند

11 In ecstasy, as if spelled by his beauty,
They were overwhelmed, made senseless.

۱۲. نشان زندگی در خود ندیدند   تُرنج و دست را درهم بریدند

12 Feeling no signs of life within themselves,
They cut their own fingers along with the oranges.

۱۳. چنان مُستغرقِ آن حور گشتند   که از هستی خود اندر گذشتند

13 So lost were they become in his beauty,
That they fell unconscious of their state.

۱۴. ز زخم آن تُرنج ودستِ پرخون   بگشت آن دلبران را جامه پُرخون

14 The orange cut, their hands red, blood dripping,
The maidens' garments were thus stained.

۱۵. بگفتند حاشَ الله این بشرنیست   جمالش جز فروغ ماه وخور نیست

15 They said, By God! This is no mortal human,
His beauty is naught but the glow of sun and moon.

۱۶. فرشته است او و یا حوربهشت است   نهالش را بنی آدم نکِشت است

16 Is he an angel, or a fair fairy from Paradise?
This sapling springs not from the seed of man.

אנדאכ'תן מאדר מוסי עליה אלסלאם רא דר אתש סוזאן אז תרס פ'רעון לעין
انداختن مادر، موسی علیه السلام را در آتش سوزان از ترس فرعون لعین
Moses is Thrown into the Fire by His Mother out of Fear of the Evil Pharaoh[5]

1. בה כ'אנה דר נבוד אן לחצ'ה עמראן   בגל כארי ב'ד או ג'מגין וחייראן
2. ג̤ו יוכבד שניד אז הוש רפ'תש   תו גויי צבר ועקל והוש רפ'תש
3. תנורי בודש אנדר כ'אנה סוזאן   מיאן אן תנור אתש פ'רוזאן
4. כלים טפל רא מאננד אספנד   רבודש מאדר ודר אתש אפ'כנד
5. דר אן בודנד כה סרהנגאן רסידנד   גשאדנד אן דר ובר ויי דו'ידנד
6. בכ'אנה דר טלב ברדנד בסיאר   נדידנד כודך אנג̣א היג̤ דיאר
7. קו'י גרם אמדנד אן נאבכאראן   ו'לי ג̤ון יד' שדנד אן כ'אכסאראן
8. בסי ג̣סתנד אנדר ו'יי נדידנד   שתאבאן נזד פ'רעון רה ברידנד
9. ג̤ו סרהנגאן שדנד אז פיש מרים   נט'ר סוי תנור אפ'כנד דר דם
10. כה תא בינד בראדר בר ג̤ה חאל אסת   ג̤גונה אכ'תרש אנדר ו'באל אסת
11. בה כ'שכי בר ג̤ו מאהי מיטפידש   זנאגה ג̤ון דראן כ'וש כ'וש בדידש
12. תנור ונאר בא גלזאר גשתה   ריאחינש ז סר תא פא גד'שתה
13. נט'ר כרדש במאדר גפ'ת מרים   ביא בנגר זמאני צ'נע אכרם
14. יקותיאל רא בין דר דל נאר   שדה אתש בר או רייחאן וגלזאר
15. ז מרים ג̤ון כה באנו אן שנידש   בג̣סת אז ג̣א ופ'רזנדש בדידש
16. ג̤ו אן חאלת בדידש ג̣פ'ת עמראן   בברדש סג̣דה אז בהר ג̣האנבאן
17. בה אמר כרדגאר פאך בי ג̤ון   בר אורדנדש אז גלזאר בירון
18. בה הם גפ'תנד ג̤ה באשד ג̤ארה כאר   נבאשד תא שונד ואקף' ז אסראר
19. ביאינד באמדאדאן באר דיגר   ביאבנד אן ג̣פ'אכאראן מנכר
20. כה מא רא אן לעינאן דר כמיננד   ביאינד נאגהי או רא בבינגד
21. בה זיר תיג'מאן ג'אפ'ל דר ארנד   בה יך סאעת דמאר אז מא בר ארנד
22. ג̤ו אז מאדר שניד או זאר בגריסת   ג̤נין גפ'תש כה אכנון ג̤ארה בר ג̤יסת
23. בה צנדוקי נהימש גפ'ת מאדר   דר אנדאזים דר ג'רקאבש אנדר
24. ז באנו ג̤ונכה מרים אן שנידש   בג̣ז אן ג̤ארהי דיגר נדידש
25. ג̣גר פ'ר כ'ון יכי צנדוק מחכם   ביאו'רדש נהאדש פיש דרדם
26. סר צנדוק רא אז הם גשאדנד   כלים אללאה רא דר ויי נהאדנד

۱. بخانه در نبود آن لحظه عَمران   بگِل کاری بُد او غمگین و حیران

1 At that time ‘Emrān was not at home,
Depressed and beleaguered, he was working with clay.

۲. چو یوکِبِد شنید از هوش رفتش   توگوئی صبر و عقل و هوش رفتش

2 When Jochebed heard the news, she lost consciousness,[6]
As if she'd lost all patience, reason, and intelligence.

5 Netzer, *Montakhab*, p. 13: *Musānāmeh* by Shāhīn.

6 Jochebed is the legendary name for the mother of Moses (Legend of the Jews: The Birth of Moses).

۳. تنوری بودش اندر خانه سوزان   میان آن تنور آتش فروزان

3 In her house there was a burning oven,
And a raging fire within the oven.

۴. کلیم طفل را مانند اِسپند   ربودش مادر و در آتش افکند

4 The mother grabbed Baby Moses,
like a grain of wild rue and threw him in the fire.

۵. درآن بودند که سرهنگان رسیدند   گشادند آن در و بر وی دویدند

5 While she was doing so, the officials arrived,
thrust the door wide open and ran to her.

۶. به خانه در طلب بردند بسیار   ندیدند کودک آنجا هیچ دیار

6 They searched the house extensively,
But no child could they see there, none.

۷. قوی گرم آمدند آن نابکاران   ولی چون یخ شدند آن خاکساران

7 Wicked men entered, hot and determined,
But they grew frigid as ice.

۸. بسی جستند اندر وی ندیدند   شتابان نزد فرعون ره بریدند

8 They searched thoroughly but could not find Moses,
So they returned straight forth to the Pharaoh.

۹. چو سرهنگان شدند از پیش مریم   نظر سوی تنور افکند در دم

9 Just as officials were leaving, Miryam,
Looked towards the oven in haste.

۱۰. که تا بیند برادر برچه حال است   چگونه اخترش اندر وبال است

10 To see how her brother was,
what fate had done to his body and limbs.

۱۱. به خشکی برچوماهی می طپیدش   ز ناگه چون درآن خوش خوش بدیدش

11 Her heart was pounding like a fish out of water,
But when she looked inside she found him alright.

۱۲. تنور و نار با گلزار گشته   ریاحینش ز سرتا پا گذشته

12 The oven and fire had turned into a flower garden,
sweet fragrance spreading all over.

۱۳. نظر کردش به مادر گفت مریم   بیا بنگر زمانی صُنع اکرم

13 Approaching her mother, Miryam said:
"Come and look for a moment at the Lord's miracle."

۱۴. یقوتیئل را بین در دل نار   شده آتش بر او ریحان و گلزار[7]

14 See baby Moses in the heart of the fire,
Look how fire has turned into a garden of roses!

۱۵. ز مریم چونکه بانو آن شنیدش   بجست از جا وفرزندش بدیدش

15 When the lady heard that from Miryam,
She ran and saw her child.

7 The Hebrew name "יקותיאל"/Yeghutiel, "یقوتیئل" is another name for Moses.

۱۶. چوآن حالت بدیدش جُفت عَمران   ببردش سُجده از بهر جهانبان
16 When Amran's spouse saw what had happened,
She bowed to the Lord of the Universe.

۱۷. به امر کردگار پاک بی چون   برآوردندش از گلزار بیرون
17 By the divine order of the Lord, peerless and pure,
They picked him from the flower garden.

۱۸. به هم گفتند چه باشد چارهٔ کار   نباشد تا شوند واقف زاسرار
18 They asked each other, "What should our plan be,
So none will find aught about this secret?"

۱۹. بیایند بامدادان بار دیگر   بیابند آن جفا کاران منکر
19 They may come again in the morning,
Those cruel non-believers, to find out.

۲۰. که ما را آن لعینان درکمینند   بیایند ناگهی او را ببینند
20 For those evil ones are lying in wait for us,
They may come without notice and find him.

۲۱. به زیر تیغمان غافل در آرند   به یک ساعت دمار از ما بر آرند
21 They'll put us to sword unawares,
And will annihilate us all at once.

۲۲. چوازمادرشنید او زار بگریست   چنین گفتش که اکنون چاره بر چیست
22 When Miryam heard this from her mother, she burst into tears,
Asking her what the solution might be.

۲۳. به صندوقی نهیمش گفت مادر   در اندازیم در غرقابش اندر
23 "We shall put him in a box," said her mother,
"And cast him onto the rushing river."

۲۴. ز بانو چونکه مریم آن شنیدش   بجز آن چارهٔ دیگر ندیدش
24 When Miryam heard this,
She saw no other way out.

۲۵. جگرپرخون یکیصندوق محکم   بیاوردش نهادش پیش در دم
25 With a bleeding heart, she brought forth,
A solid box and placed it before her mother.

۲۶. سر صندوق را از هم گشادند   کلیم الله را در وی نهادند
26 Opening the lid of the box,
They put "the Lord's interlocutor" inside.

חמל כרדן צנדוק עהד
حمل کردن صندوق عهد
The Transfer of the Ark of the Covenant[8]

1. בגפ'ת איך ובכוהנאן בפ'רמוד   כה ברדאריד ארון רא זגׄא זוד
2. רויד אנדר סוי ירדן שתאבאן   גׄנין שוד אמר גׄבבאר גׄהאנבאן

8 'Emrāni, *Fatḥnāmeh*, ms. BZI 964: 23b.

3. פס אנגה הר גֶה חק פ'רמודה בודש   בכוהנאן וכ'אצאן ו'א נמודש
4. גֶו כוהנאן שנידנד אמר דאור   נהאדנד גִמלגי תווראת בר סר
5. רו'אן גשתנת סוי ירדן כ'ראמאן   בני יעקוביאן דר פיי שתאבאן
6. גִו'אן ו טפ'ל ו פיר ו כ'רד ו מהתר   בזרג ו כוגֶך ו דרו'יש ו סרו'ר
7. ש'דנד דנבאל כוהנאן רו'אנה   בה צדק פאך בי ע' ד'ר ובהאנה
8. המי רפ'תנד כוהנאן כ'ראמאן   בה פישאפיש בא תווראת וארון
9. פיי אישאן המי רפ'תנד יכ סר   בני יעקוביאן אז פ'רמאן דאור
10. רסידנד כוהנאן גֶון בר לב אב   ז הר גִאנב שתאבאן דר תך ותאב
11. נאיסתאדנד בר גִא אן דליראן   נהאדנד גאם באב אן רה שיראן
12. ז אמר פאדשאה פאדשאהאן   כ'טא בכ'ש גִהאן פ'ר גנאהאן
13. גֶו פאי כוהנאן אז כ'אך בר אב   רסיד אז ק'דרת ו תקדיר והאב
14. זהם בשכאפת אן בחר ה'מאיון   תו גויי בחר ירדן ש'ד גֶו האמון
15. הראן אבי כה דר ירדן שתאבאן   המי אמד ז הר רודי פ'ראואן

۱. بگفت این و بکوهنان بفرمود   که بر دارید آرون را ز جا زود

1 He said this and ordered the priests:
"Lift the Ark of the Covenant with haste."

۲. روید اندر سوی یردن شتابان   چنین شد امر جبّار جهانبان

2 "Go quickly towards Jordan,"
This was the order of the Almighty keeper of the world.

۳. پس آنگه هرچه حق فرموده بودش   به کوهنان و خاصان وا نمودش

3 Then whatever the Lord had commanded him,
He related to the priests and the noblemen.

۴. چو کوهنان شنیدند امر داور   نهادند جملگی تورات بر سر

4 Once the priests heard the Lord's orders,
Together, they all placed the Torah on their heads.

۵. روان گشتند سوی یردن خرامان   بنی یعقوبیان در پی شتابان

5 Towards Jordan they set out with grace,
Followed swiftly by the Israelites.

۶. جوان و طفل وپیروخرد و مهتر   بزرگ وکوچک و درویش و سرور

6 Young and old, high and low,
Grand and minor, poor and mighty.

۷. شدند دنبال کوهنان روانه   به صدق پاک بی عذر و بهانه

7 They followed the priests wholeheartedly,
In all honesty, with no excuses or complaints.

۸. همی رفتند کوهنان خرامان   به پیشاپیش با تورات و آرون

8 The priests marched with grace,
Walking ahead with the Torah and the Ark.

۹. پی ایشان همی رفتند یک سر   بنی یعقوب از فرمان داور

9 The Israelites trailed behind them all together,
Just as the Lord had commanded.

۱۰. رسیدند کوهنان چون برلب آب   زهرجانب شتابان درتک و تاب

10 As the priests reached the water’s edge,
They all bustled with excitement.

۱۱. نایستادند بر جا آن دلیران   نهادند پا به آب آن نَره شیران

11 Those brave ones did not hesitate,
Stepping into the waters, those fearless lions.

۱۲. ز امر پادشاه پادشاهان   خطا بخش جهانِ پُر گناهان

12 Following the order of the King of Kings,
The One who forgives the sinners of the world,

۱۳. چو پای کوهنان از خاک بر آب   رسید از قدرت و تقدیر وهّاب

13 As the priests’ feet crossed from land to water,
By the Lord’s grace, power and will.

۱۴. زهم بشکافت آن بحر همایون   تو گوئی بحریردن شد چوهامون

14 The grand sea split asunder,
As if the Jordan Sea had turned into a plain.

۱۵. هرآن آبی که در یردن شتابان   همی آمد ز هر رودی فراوان

15 All the water rushed out of Jordan,
And gushed into the sea from every river.

רפ'תן שמשון בר מלך פלשתים ו דידן אן ד'כ'תראן קומאן אז באב פלשתים ו עאשק ש'דן או ו כ"שתן או אן נרה שיר רא פ'רמאיד

رفتن شمشون بر مُلک پلشطیم و دیدن آن دخترانِ قومان ازباب پلشطیم عاشق شدن او و کشتنِ او آن نره شیر را فرماید

Samson’s Visit to the Land of Peleshtim, His Acquaintance with the Maidens of the Peleshtim Tribe, His Falling in Love, and His Killing of a Male Lion[9]

1. ביא בשנוו כה שמשון דאו'ר   גֶה הא כרד או אבא קוומאן כאפ'ר
2. גְו'אני בוד' האמגֶו סרו' ו רענא   המי גשתי בה אשתאול וצארעא
3. כ"דא רא בוד בא או בס שפ'אעת   בדאד או רא דלירי ו ש'גְאעת
4. אגר כה רו נהאדי או אבר כוה   בה יך סאעת בכנדי כוה אנבוה
5. וגר שיר אומדי אנדר ג'ד'ארש   בה תעגִיל או ש'די אנדר כנארש
6. זנכ'דאנש גרפ'תי בא לבאנש   בה הם בשכאפתי ר דם דהאנש
7. דו'ידי אז פייאש בי גֶוב וזנגִיר   כה תא אן שיר רא כרדי נכ'גִיר
8. דרידי תא כמר גאהש גֶו כרבאס   יגֶו כ'ייאטאן כה גֶידנדש ז מקראצ
9. דלירי בוד או בא הייבת ובים   המי רפ'ת או בה סר חד פלשתים
10. אגר גֶה סלטנת בודי בה אישאן   ולי בודנד זבים או פרישאן
11. קצ'א רוזי המי גרדיד שאדאן   בה לשכרגאה אן קוומאן נאדאן
12. כה דיד או נאגהי אנדר כ'יאבאן   נשסתה ד'כ'תרי גֶון מאה תאבאן

9 Aharon Ben Mashiaḥ Isfahani, *Shofṭimnāmeh*, ms. BZI 964, ff. 160b–161a.

13. וליכן בוד אז קוום פלשטים — כה בודי פ'תנהאי אז בהר אקלים
14. גִו או רא דיד שמשון דלאו'ר — בש'ד חייראן בר ו'יי אן ג'ט'נפ'ר
15. בשד עאשק בר ו'יי המגִו מאהש — ביאפ'תאד אתשי אנדר כלאהש
16. כה בוד או ד'כ'תרי נג'ז ו לטיפ'י — נגארי מהו'שי שוכ'י ט'ריפ'י
17. גִמאלש בוד המגִו נאר ופנבה — תו גויי בוד המגִו נאן וד'נבה
18. גִו שמשון רא נמאנדי צברו תאבש — ביאמד אן דם פיש באבש
19. בה באבש ג'פ'ת ב'ו'ד אין ארזוים — המי כ'ואהם כה אכנון בא תו גוים
20. רו'אן גשתם מן אז סר חד תימנא — בדידם ד'כ'תרי גִון סרו' רענא
21. בדידם יך נט'ר או רא מן אז דור — נדאנם מן פרי בוד או ו' יא חור
22. ש'דם שיידא גִו זאן כרדם נגאהי — המי כ'ואהם ו'רא בהרם בכ'ואהי
23. גִו מאבווה שניד אז ו'יי ס'כ'ן רא — בה רוי תרביית ג'פ'תי פסר רא
24. כה אין נאלאיק אסת איי נור דידה — ז כ'יישאנם המה הסתנד גזידה
25. ב'ו'נד אן הר יכי מאננד מאהי — ביא בא מן הר אן שכ'צי כה כ'ואהי

۱. بیا بشنو که شمشونِ داور — چه ها کرد او اَبا قومان کافر

1 Come and hear about Samson the Judge,
About how he treated the blasphemer tribes.

۲. جوانی بود همچو سرو و رعنا — همی گشتی به اِشتائول و صارعا

2 He was a young man, handsome and tall as a cedar,
He traveled to Eshtaol and Zorah.[10]

۳. خدا را بود با او بس شفاعت — بداد او را دلیری و شجاعت

3 The Lord intervened for him many a time,
And bestowed courage and bravery upon him.

۴. اگر که رو نهادی او آبر کوه — به یک ساعت بکندی کوهِ انبوه

4 If he was going towards a huge mountain,
He would upend that massive mountain in a flash.

۵. وگر شیر اومدی اندر گذارش — به تعجیل او شدی اندر کنارش

5 If there were a lion in his way,
He would rush up beside it.

۶. زنخدانش گِرفتی با لبانش — بهم بشکافتی در دم دهانش

6 Grab its chin and lips,
And tear open its mouth in an instant.

۷. دویدی از پِیَش بی چوب و زنجیر — که تا آن شیر را کردی نخجیر

7 He would run after it, with no stick or chain,
Until he hunted it down.

۸. دریدی تا کمرگاهش چو کرباس — چوخیاطان‌که‌چیدندش‌ز مقراض

8 He would tear it to its waist like cloth,
Just like the tailors cut with scissors.

10 Zorah and Eshtaol (Judges: 13:24): the names of sites in the foothills, southeast of Jerusalem (*Oxford Annotated Bible*).

۹. دلیری بود او با هیبت و بیم   همی رفت او به سر حدّ پلشطیم

9 He was a brave man with a terrifying aspect,
He went to the borders of Pelishtim.[11]

۱۰. اگر چه سلطنت بودی به ایشان   ولی بودند زبیم او پریشان

10 Although they were the rulers,
The people were anxious and fearful of him.

۱۱. قضا روزی همی گردید شادان   به لشکرگاه آن قومان نادان

11 One day, by fate, he chanced upon,
The camp of those ignorant people.

۱۲. که دید او ناگهی اندر خیابان   نشسته دختری چون ماه تابان

12 Unexpectedly did he see in the street,
A maiden sitting, shining like the moon.

۱۳. ولیکن بود از قوم پلشطیم   که بودی فتنه ای از بهر اقلیم

13 But she was from the people of Pelishtim,
Where there was a disturbance across the land.

۱۴. چو او را دید شَشمونِ دلاور   بشد حیران بر وی آن غضنفر

14 That lion-hearted Samson, the hero,
Was mesmerized when he saw her.

۱۵. بشد عاشق بروی همچو ماهش   بیفتاد آتشی اندر کلاهش

15 He fell in love with her moon-like face,
A burning flame was kindled in his heart.

۱۶. که بود او دختری نغز و لطیفی   نگاری مهوشی، شوخی، ظریفی

16 A maiden, sweet and tender,
A beloved beauty, jocund and delicate.

۱۷. جمالش بود همچو نار و پنبه   تو گویی بود همچو نان و دنبه

17 Her complexion was like fire and cotton,
So soft she was, and plump like buttered bread.

۱۸. چو شِمشون را نماندی صبر و تابش   بیامد آندم پیش بابش

18 As Samson lost all patience and calm,
He went to his father without delay.

۱۹. به بابش گفت بُوَد این آرزویم   همی خواهم که اکنون با تو گویم

19 He told his father what his wish was:
"I want to tell you now," he said,

۲۰. روان گشتم من از سَر حدّ تیمنا   بدیدم دختری چون سرو رعنا

20 "As I was passing by the borders of Timnah,
I saw a girl tall and trimmed like a cypress."[12]

11 Peleshtim (Philistine Judges: 14): one of a people of Aegean origin who settled on the southern coast of Palestine in the 12th century BCE, about the time of the arrival of the Israelites. https://www.britannica.com/topic/Philistine-people. (Accessed June 7, 2020)

12 Timnah is "A town on the northern border of Judah (Joshua 15:10), lying between Beth-shemesh and Ekron. It is probably the same Timnah as Judah visited (Genesis 38:12–14), and certainly the scene of Samson's adventures (Judges 14:1); his 'father-in-law' is called a 'Timnite' (Judges 15:6)". https://www.biblestudytools.com/dictionary/timnah/:(accessed April 12, 2020)

۲۱. بدیدم یک نظر او را من از دور   ندانم من پری بود او و یا حور

21 "I only caught a glimpse of her from afar,
I know not if she was an angel or a fairy."

۲۲. شدم شیدا چو زان کردم نگاهی   همی خواهم وِرا بهرم بخواهی

22 "I was enthralled by a single glance at her,
I want to ask you for her hand."

۲۳. چو مانوَخ شنید از وی سخن را   به روی تربیت گفتی پسر را

23 When Manoah heard these words from him,
For counsel he told the son:

۲۴. که این نالایق است ای نور دیده   ز خویشانم همه هستند گزیده

24 "She will not do, O light of my eyes.
My family members are all of the Chosen People."

۲۵. بُوَند آن هر یکی مانند ماهی   بیا با من هر آن شخصی که خواهی

25 "Each one of whom possesses moon-like radiance,
Come with me, and choose whichever maiden you wish".

מסלחת כרדן דאריוש עראקי ו כור'ש פארסי דר מגִלס מיי ו עזם רפ'תן בר סר בלשאצר בסוי בג'דאד

مصلحت کردن داریوش عراقی و کورش پارسی در مجلس می و عزم رفتن بر سر بلشاصر بسوی بغداد

The Consultation between Dariush the Babylonian and Cyrus the Persian at a Wine-Drinking Gathering and the Resolution to Attack Baghdad via Belshazzar[13]

1. קצ'א רא דאריוש שאה מאדי   בה כור'ש ג'פ'ת דר כייפ'יית מיי
2. כה או'רדה אסת פייכי תיז גאמי   ז בג'דאד אז בראי מן פיאמי
3. ז כאר ובאר שאהי ניסת אגאה   כהשאהאןמרדהאנדואושדהשאה
4. כהפורב'כ'תאלנצראןשאהבדנאם   בה תכ'ת סלטנת בגרפ'תה אראם
5. נמידאנד טריק מ'לך דארי   נה דר גִנג אסת מרד כאר זארי
6. פ'סון וחילה שאהאן גֶה דאנד   בדניא תא כה ע'מרי נגד'ראנד
7. בזיר ח'כמש אן כשו'ר דריג' אסת   במיידאנש סרש לאיק בתיג' אסת
8. רו'אן באיד ש'ד אכנון בר סר או   כה אכנון הסת ג'אפ'ל לשכר או
9. אז או גירים שהרסתאן בג'דאד   בר אנדאזימש אז אפ'אק בניאד
10. שו'ים אלקצה בר דשמן מ'ט'פ'פ'ר   ערוס מלך רא גירים דר בר
11. שו'ד חאצל אז או כאם דל מא   המין באשד זשאהי חאצל מא
12. שהנשה רא גֶו כורש בוד דאמאד   בנאגֶארי בה תדבירש רט'א דאד
13. בה בלשצר כ'יאל רזם כרדנד   בה רפתן בר סר או עזם כרדנד

۱. قضا را داریوش شاه مادی   به کورش گفت در کیفیّت می

1 The Median King Daryush once,
Told Cyrus, while drunk with wine:

13 Netzer, *Montakhab*, p. 262: *Dāniālnāmeh* (The Book of Daniel) by Khāwjeh Bukhara'i.

۲. که آورده است پیکی تیزگامی ز بغداد از برای من پیامی

2 "A fleet-footed messenger has brought,
News to me from Baghdad."

۳. ز کار و بار شاهی نیست آگاه که شاهان مرده اند و او شده شاه

3 "He is not aware of the rules of kingship,
Since all the kings were dead when he became king."

۴. که پورِ بُخت النصر آن شاهِ بَد نام به تختِ سلطنت بگرفته آرام

4 "That the son of Nebuchadnezzar, the infamous despot,
Has found peace upon the royal throne."

۵. نمیداند طریق مُلک داری نه در جنگ است، مرد کارزاری

5 "But does he know how to rule,
Nor does he act as a hero on the battlefield."

۶. فسون و حیلهٔ شاهان چه داند به دنیا تا که عمری نگذراند

6 "What can he know of the duplicity of kings
Until he grows much older and more seasoned?"

۷. بزیر حکمش آن کشوردریغ است به میدانش سرش لایق به تیغ است

7 "It is a pity for that country to be under his rule,
He deserves to be beheaded in the city square."

۸. روان باید شد اکنون بر سر او که اکنون هست غافل لشکراو

8 "An attack must be launched upon him now,
Since his army is off guard at the moment."

۹. از او گیریم شهرستان بغداد بر اندازیمش از آفاق بنیاد

9 "We should capture the city of Baghdad from him,
And wipe him out from all horizons!"

۱۰. شویم القصه بر دشمن مظفّر عروس ملک را گیریم در بر

10 "Once we are victorious over the enemy,
We shall bring that kingdom-bride into our embrace!"

۱۱. شود حاصل از او کام دل ما همین باشد ز شاهی حاصل ما

11 "Our wishes shall be fulfilled, through him,
From his kingdom, our benefit shall be gained."

۱۲. شهنشه را چو کورش بود داماد به ناچاری به تدبیرش رضا داد

12 As the King of Kings had Cyrus for a son-in-law,
He was obliged to consent to his plans.

۱۳. به بلشاصر خیال رزم کردند به رفتن بر سر اوعزم کردند

13 Intending to wage battle against Belshazzar,
They started out, determined upon their attack.

כתאב רות
کتاب روت
Book of Ruth[14]

1. בה בת לחם יהודא בוד גֻואני ז שבטאי יהודא כאמראני

14 'Emrāni, *Fatḥnāmeh*, ms. BZI 964, f. 184b.

2. ב'ד או רא מאל ו מלך ו גֶיז בסיאר   בסי מחצול ו כשת ו כאר ואבאר
3. אלי מלך' המי גפ'תנד נאמש   בההרבאבי כ'דאבודדאדה כאמש
4. זני בודש אלי מלך' בה כ'אנה   סבק בֻרדה ז כ'ובאן זמאנה
5. בה כ'ובי אסמאנש מאה מי כ'ואנד   כהכ'ורשידאזגַמאלשבאזמימאנד
6. ברהנה מהר אגר דידי ו'גֻודש   ז גֶרך' גֶהארמין כרדי סגֻודש
7. פדר או רא נהאדה נעומי נאם   לבש גֶון שכר ו גֶשמש גֶו באדאם

۱. به بِت لِحِم یهودا بود جوانی   ز شبطای یهودا کامرانی

1 In Bethlehem lived a young man,
A lucky man from the tribe of Judah.

۲. بُد او را مال و مُلک و چیز بسیار   بسی محصول و کِشت و کار و انبار

2 He possessed ample treasure, property, and belongings,
And many cultivated crops in his stores and silos.

۳. اِلی مِلِخ همی گفتند نامش   به هر بابی خدا بود داده کامش

3 Eli Meleck was the name he went by,
And the Lord had bestowed upon him great fortune.

۴. زنی بودش اِلی مِلِخ به خانه   سبق بُرده ز خوبانِ زمانه

4 Eli Meleck had a wife at home,
Whose beauty had surpassed any beauty of her time.

۵. به خوبی آسمانش ماه می خواند   که خورشید از جمالش باز می ماند

5 The sky called her the moon for her beauty,
Her loveliness even awed the sun.[15]

۶. برهنه مهر اگر دیدی وجودش   ز چرخ چهارمین کردی سجودش

6 If the sun viewed her beauty unveiled,
It would fall prostrate before her from the fourth firmament.

۷. پدر او را نهاده نَعُومی نام   لبش چون شکر و چشمش چو بادام

7 Her father had named her Naomi,
Her lips were sugary and her eyes like almonds.

חנוכא נאמה עמראני
حنوکا نامه عمرانی
Ḥannukahnāmeh of ‘Emrāni[16]

1. דר מיקדאש גִמלה בגשאדנד   המה אסבאב כ'אץ בנהאדנד
2. המה אסבאבהא מ'הייא בוד   ג'יר אז אן רווג'ן כה נאפידא בוד
3. רווג'ן זיית כ'אץ מיבאיסת   ג'יר אז אן רווג'ני נמישאיסת
4. דר עזארא בסי בגרדידנד   רווג'ן זיית، שישהאי דידנד
5. כוהנים אנדר או ש'דנד דלשאד   כה כ'דא כאם אן עזיזאן דאד

15 The sun is one of the seven spheres of the universe. According to *Loghatnameh-ye Dehkhoda*, it is the fourth sphere.
[فرهنگ دهخدا: چرخ چهارم ” کنایه از خورشید جهان فروز“ است].

16 ‘Emrāni, *Ḥanukāhnāmeh*, ms. BZI 2075, ff. 53a–54b.

6. גֶון מתתיא בדיד אן רווג'ן   כרד המה גֶראג'הא רווושן
7. אנקדר בוד תא שבי סוזד   כ'אנה כ'אץ רא בר אפ'רוזד
8. בישתר זאן נבוד רוג'ן כ'אץ   גֶון בר אפ'רוכת אז סר אכ'לאץ
9. חק תעאלא בה כורי דשמן   תא בה השת רוז כרד אן רושן
10. שאם תא צבח ו צבח תא שאם   בוד רווושן גֶראג'הא מאדאם
11. תא כה תרתיב רווג'ן זייתון   סאכתנד אז כראמת בי גֶון
12. אן עגִאיב כה דיד איסראיל   המה חיראן ש'דה בה קדרת אל
13. גֶון גֶבין קדרתי עיאן דידנד   המה אז גִאן בה חק בנאלידנד
14. המה דל בא כ'דאו'נד בסתנד   אז דל וגִאן בה דוסת פיו'סתנד

۱. در میقداش جمله بگشادند   همه اسباب خاّص بنهادند

1 They re-opened the gate of the Temple,
Rearranged all the special devices.

۲. همه اسبابها مهیا بود   غیر از آن روغن که ناپیدا بود

2 All the utensils were prepared,
Except the oil, which could not be found.

۳. روغَنِ زیتِ خاصّ مي بایست   غیر از آن روغنی نمی شایست

3 A special olive oil was needed,
No other oil would be suitable to use.

۴. دَر عِزارا بسی بگردیدند   روغنِ زیت، شیشه ای دیدند

4 Searching everywhere in the chambers of the Temple,
They found a jar of the right olive oil.

۵. کوهنیم اندر او شدند دلشاد   که خدا کام آن عزیزان داد

5 This delighted the priest,
Joyful for the Lord making their wish come true.

۶. چون مَتتیا بدید آن روغن   کرد همه چراغها روشن

6 Once Mattathias saw all that oil,
He lit all the lamps.[17]

۷. آنقدر بود تا شبی سوزد   خانهٔ خاص را بر افروزد

7 The oil was only enough to burn for one night,
Lighting up that special place

۸. بیشتر زان نبود روغن خاص   چون برافروخت از سَرِ اخلاص

8 Knowing there was not much of that special oil,
Once it was lit up with pure devotion.

۹. حقّ تعالی به کوری دشمن   تا به هشت روز گرد آن روشن

9 The Exalted Lord, in opposition to the enemy,
Kept the lights burning for eight days.

17 Mattathias, (died *c.* 166 BC), Jewish priest and landowner of Modein, near Jerusalem, who defied the decree of Antiochus IV Epiphanes of Syria to Hellenize the Jews; he fled to the Judaean hills with his five sons and waged a guerrilla war against the Syrians, being succeeded by his son Judas Maccabeus. https://www.britannica.com/biography/Mattathias. (Accessed April 9, 2020)

۱۰. شام تا صبح و صبح تا شام   بود روشن چراغ ها مادام

10 Dusk to dawn and dawn to dusk,
All the time the lanterns were burning.

۱۱. تا که ترتیبِ روغنِ زیتون   ساختند از کرامَتِ بی چون

11 Until finally, the oil was spent,
With the grace of the Lord.

۱۲. از عجایب که دید ایسراییل   همه حیران شده به قدرتِ اِل

12 From this miracle that the Israelites saw,
All were awed by the His power.[18]

۱۳. چون چنین قدرتی عیان دیدند   همه از جان به حقّ بنالیدند

13 Once this power was apparent to them,
All heartily supplicated themselves to the Lord.

۱۴. همه دِل با خداوند بستند   از دِل و جان به دوست پیوستند

14 All pledged allegiance to the Lord,
And wholeheartedly joined that Beloved.

דאסתאן חננא ו' הפת בראדראן
מויה גפתן פסר או'לין בראי כישתן
داستان حنا و هفت برادران
مویه گفتن پسر اولین برای خویشتن
The Story of Ḥanna and the Seven Brothers: Lamentation of the First Son for Himself[19]

1.	איא מאדר חלאלם כן חלאלם	כה מן דר מחנת ו רנגֿ ו זו'אלם
2.	בה דסת כאפ'ראן אכנון בזארי	נדארם היגֶֿונה רסתגארי
3.	דריג'א דר בלאי גֿאו'דאני	פ'תאדימאן יכאיך נאגהאני
4.	גֶֿה סאזם גֿון כנם גֶֿארה נדארם	בה נאגאהי סר אמד רוזגארם
5.	דריג'א אז גֿו'אני בר נכ'ורדים	בה סר זארי ו סר אנדוהי מרדים
6.	בדסת כאפ'ראן גשתם גרפ'תאר	גֶֿה סאזם גֿון נדארם גֶֿארה כאר
7.	זמן בדרוד באש איי מאדר פיר	כה בא תקדיר יזדאן ניסת תדביר
8.	דלאזמן בר כן איי מאדר בה יך באר	נכ'אהי דיד מרא זנדה דגר רבאר
9.	בגפ'ת ו דאדראן בגרפ'ת דר בר	ז גריה כרד רוי יך ביך תר
10.	בה זארי גפ'ת בא אן דלפ'גאראן	איא ביגֶֿארגאן ו ביקראראן
11.	מבאדא גֿון מרא אז פא דר ארנד	דמאר אז גֿאן מא יעני בר ארנד
12.	שמארא דל שו'ד אשכסתה נאגאה	מסאל כאפ'ראן גרדיד גמראה
13.	גֶֿו באיד רפ'ת אז אין דנאי בנאכאם	המאן בהתר כה באשים מא נכו נאם
14.	נמירד הרכה נאמש ניך באשד	ז בד דור ו בה קח נזדיך באשד

18 The Hebrew term “אל” (El/اِل) is a reference to the Lord.

19 Netzer, *Montakhab*, p. 232, The story of Ḥannaa and Seven Brothers (2 Maccabees 7:1–42) by ‘Emrāni.

۱. ایا مادر حلالم کن حلالم   که من در محنت و رنج و زوالم

1 O Mother, pardon me, give pardon,
For I am in pain, suffering and demise.

۲. به دست کافران اکنون بزاری   ندارم هیچگونه رستگاری

2 At the hands of unbelievers I am in despair,
I do not see any way to redemption.

۳. دریغا در بلای جاودانی   فتادیمان یکایک ناگهانی

3 Alas, we have fallen into this eternal misfortune,
One by one, unexpectedly.

۴. چه سازم چون کنم چاره ندارم   به نا گاهی سر آمد روزگارم

4 What can I do? I have no recourse,
My life came to an end with no warning.

۵. دریغا از جوانی بر نخوردیم   به سر زاری و سر اندوهی مردیم

5 Alas, we took no pleasure in our youth,
Instead we died in misery and sorrow.

۶. بدست کافران گشتم گرفتار   چه سازم چون ندارم چاره کار

6 I have been trapped in the hands of unbelievers,
What to do, when I have no way out

۷. ز من بدرود باش ای مادر پیر   که با تقدیرِ یزدان نیست تدبیر

7 Bid me farewell, O aged mother,
Since there is no release from divine destiny.

۸. دل از من بر کن ای مادر به یک بار   نخواهی دید مرا زنده دگر بار

8 Give me up, O Mother, for good,
For you shall not see me alive again.

۹. بگفت و دادران بگرفت در بر   ز گریه کرد روی یک به یک تر

9 Saying this, he embraced his brothers,
They shed tears on each other's faces.

۱۰. به زاری گفت با آن دل فگاران   آ یا بیچار گان و بیقراران

10 In agony, he addressed the distressed,
The helpless and the restless.

۱۱. مبادا چون مرا از پا در آرند   دمار از جان ما یعنی برآرند

11 Once I am cut down heaven forbid,
Meaning of my life is terminated.

۱۲. شما را دل شود اِشکسته ناگاه   مثال کافران گردید گمراه

12 May you not be heartbroken at once,
And like the unbelievers, stray from the path.

۱۳. چو باید رفت ازین دنیا بنا کام   همان بهترکه باشیم ما نکو نام

13 When one has to leave this world unfulfilled,
We might as well leave with a reputable name.

۱۴. نمیرد هر که نامش نیک باشد   زبد دور و بحق نزدیک باشد

14 Never dies, the one honored with good name,
He who stands far from evil and close to truth.

Historical Poetry

כתאב אנוסי
מסלמאן כרדן שאה עבאס איסראילאן אצפ'האן רא
كتاب انوسی
مسلمان كردن شاه عباس ایسرائلان اصفهان را

وقایع دوران ۱۶۱۳–۱۶۶۰ میلادی

Ketāb-e Anūsi: The Forced Conversion of Shah Abbas and the Jews of Isfahan(1613–1660)[20]

1. ג'צ'ב ש'ד שאה ו אתש בר גִהאן ריכ'ת   המה קהר בר סר ישראילאן ריכ'ת
2. תמאמי רא טלב כרד ובפ'רמוד   כה דר תוראת בנו'שת מעבוד
3. מ'חמד גֶו ט'הור איד בעאלם   ש'מא גרדיד בר דינש מ'סללם
4. כנון אז ו'עדה גֶנדין סאל בגד'שת   מסלמאנתאן המי באיד כנון גשת
5. אגר יך יך בגויתאן שהאדת   המה יאביד דר ד'ניא סעאדת
6. אגר נה המגֶו מלאתאן המין דם   שמא רא מיפ'רסתם דרגִהנם
7. אלאהי היגֶ כס או רא נבינד   דר איך באג' גִהאן איך גל דביגֶב
8. סגאן אסתאדה ומ'לא פ'תאדה   שה פ'ר קהר ו סימאנטוב סתאדה
9. בתרסידנד אן ביגֶארהאי גֶנד   בלרזידנד גֶון אז גורג' גוספ'נד
10. ז רוי תרס יך יך פיש רפ'תנד   שהאדת הם בדסת שאה גופ'תנד
11. גֶו יך גֶנדי בה דסת שה מסלמאן   ש'דן ש'ד שאה אז מסתי פשימאן
12. ברפ'ת כ'וד אנדרון ודאד רכ'צת   ו'זיר כ'יש רא גפ'ת או בה חרמת
13. הר אנכס רא ראיס מומן ביארד   שהאדת גויד ו דר דין דר ארד
14. דגר גֶנדי ו'זירש דאדה אימאן   ו' יך גֶנדי סימאנטוב כרדה מ'סלמאן
15. נו'שתה גִמלה רא יך סר אסאמי   ב'דנד הפ'תאד ו פנג תן מרד נאמי
16. בש'ד רוז דגר מסת מיי נאב   בג'פת תוראתהא ריזנד דר אב
17. ג'לאמאן גִמלה דר מידאן דוידנד   כתאבהא גִמלה בר סר פ'ל מיכשידנד
18. תמאמי ריכ'תנד בר זנדה רודש   המה דר אב ש'סתנד חרף'ו חרופ'ש
19. גרפ'תנד רכ'צת מ'לא אבאי צדיק   בכ'אכש בספרנד אז רוי תחקיק
20. פ'לך יך כארהא רא דסת א'סתאד   דהד ביצֶארגאן רא זוד בר באד
21. צֶו און ביצֶארה דר כ'אכש ספרדנד   תמאמי גושת רא בא מאסת כ'רדנד
22. מ'סלמאני המי כרדנד נאצֶאר   דר נו'אב מירפ'תנד בה זנהאר
23. ב'די שייכ'י בה דוור אן שהנשאה   בהא אלדין אסם או תרסאי אללאה
24. בסי חרמת ב'דש דר נזד שאהאן   המי כרדנד סגִודש ספ' פנאהאן

20 Bābāi' Ben Lotf, *Ketāb-e Anūsi*, ms. BZI 917. ff. 20a–22a.

25. תמאמי כ'לק או רא מיסתודנד   בה אנגשתש בה יך דיגר מינמודנד
26. ברפ'תנד אן ג̇מאעת נזד אן מרד   בגפ'תנד שייך' דידי שה צֶהא כרד?
27. בכשת מ'לאי מא רא או בנאחק   בריכ'ת תווראת רא בר אב מ'תלק
28. צֶובשנידשייך'אינהאראבראש'פ'ת   בזד בר סר דו דסת ו יך צֶנין גפ'ת
29. כ''דאו'נדא מן אסתג'פ'אר כרדם   בג̇אי אשך דל כ'ון כאר כרדם
30. צֶנאן תווראת רא כרדנד פאמאל   צֶרא פישש המי רפ'תנד אמסאל?
31. כ'נון יך מסלחת בינם מן אז ג̇אן   כה שה איד מרא פ'רדא בה מהמאן
32. בכ'אהד מסלחת דידן אבא מן   בגושש דר ברם שאיד יכי פ'ן
33. בפאיש דר פ'תאדנד ו זאר כרדנד   ספ'ארש הר יכי בסיאר כרדנד
34. אז אנג̇א רוי נהאדנד דר גה מיר   בגופ'תנדכרדהאימאןג̇'מלהתקציר
35. רצ'אי חק בכ'ר מא רא דגר באר   בה דרגאהת שו'ים רוזי דו צד באר
36. בגופ'תש מיר מ'חמד קאסם אז כין   בגפ'תם אז כ'ר שייטאן בה פאין
37. ביאייתאן ו כ'וד צ'איע מסאזיד   ז בהר כ'ד שש ו פנג̇ מבאזיד
38. צֶו נשנידיד סכ'ן אז מן סר אנג̇אם   המי נושיד זהר אכנון צֶנאן ג̇אם
39. בגופ'תנד דיגרש אז רוי זארי   כה חק יארת בו'ד צֶון חק גד'ארי
40. ז בהר חק רסאן יך באר דיגר   סלאם מא בה באנוי דו כשו'ר
41. בגו יאראן סלאמת מירסאננד   כה מארא צֶארה סאזאכ'ר אזין בנד
42. צלאחי בהר אין ביצֶארגאן בין   ד'עא גוי תואנד אין ג̇מע מסאכין
43. בגופ'תנדאיןוברפ'תנדדלפ'ראזכ'ון   ז בהר דאת בודנד המצֶו מג̇נון
44. גֶו יך מדת בר אמד צחבת דין   ביאמדשאהנזדיךשייך'בהאאלדין
45. צֶו שייך' מ'עתבר שה דיד אז דור   סג̇ודי כרד ו אכראמי בה דסתור
46. בגפ'ת שאהא הזאראן ג̇אן פ'דאית   בה דידה מיכשם מן כ'אך פאית
47. צֶגונה ע'זר מקדומת בכ'אהם   כה מן יך בנדה אז פאדשאהם
48. בגפ'ת שאהש כה איי שייך' בצירם   מרא יך משו'רת באשד בה פירם
49. אגר סאזי א'מ̇ידו'ארם ז מחשר   אגר נה דסת זנם בר כאר דיגר
50. בגפ'תשייכ'שכהאייכ'ורשידכ'או'ר   מ'ראדת צֶיסת אז באזאר מחשר
51. בגפ'ת גבראן אבא ג̇מע יהודאן   המי כ'אהם כ'נם אינאן מ'סלמאן
52. צֶו בשניד אין סכ'ן הא שייך' אז ו'יי   בג'פת הסת המתת צֶו חאתם תיי
53. יהודאן רא ניאזארי תו זנהאר   כה פיג'מבר ספ'ארש כרד בסיאר
54. בה תכליף' ו תווראתש תא תואניד   יהודאן רא מסלמאני רסאניד
55. דגר הם כ'וד מוסאי פיאמבר   ז ג̇מע אנביא בודי כלאנתר
56. עשר איאת או או חק גרפתה   בה הר באבי סוי מעראג̇ רפתה
57. ו'לי גבראן נדארנד דין ו אימאן   בג̇ווראן מיתואני כרד מוסלמאן
58. צֶו שה בשניד אז שייך' אין רו'אית   דלש כרד אז חדית' או סראית
59. ברון אמד אז אנג̇א שד סו'ארה   סוי נו'אב ש'ד בא סד לג̇ארה
60. בדיד אנג̇א סתאדה ג̇מע עברי   נשסתה פיש אישאן מיר נ'כ'רי
61. צֶו שה אז דור דידנד אן ג̇מאעת   אבא מיר אמדנד דר סג̇דה סאעת
62. צֶו שה אישאן בדיד גפ'תא כה דיגר   בשד דאר אליהוד באז אין דר
63. פ'רוז אמד בש'ד דר פיש נו'אב   בה פאיש ש'ד רו'אן נו'אב צֶון אב

64. נשאנדש בר צף' ו בר פאש זר ריכ'ת   בכ'דמת יך זמאן צֶון שמע או'יכת
65. פס אז כ'דמת בכרדנד גופ'תגו רא   בה הר שהרי בהר ג̇אי ס'כ'נהא
66. ס'כ'ן אנדר ס'כ'ן אמד בה בירון   כה תא אמד יכי חרף' אז יהודאן
67. בה מננת כ'ואסת נו'אב עליה   כה אישאן מידהנד הר מאה ג̇זיה
68. חלאל אסת פול אישאן איי בראדר   מדה מא רא מו'אג̇ב ג̇אי דיגר
69. נהאד או מננתי בר דוש אן מאה   כהבכ'שידםבהתואיןקוםגמראה
70. אלאהי חרף' נאבי רא ביאן כון   גאולאה רא בה באבאי עיא ן כון

۱. غضب شد شاه و آتش بر جهان ریخت   همه قهر بر سر ایسرائلان ریخت

1 The king was enraged and set the world on fire,
All his wrath directed at the Israelites.

۲. تمامی را طلب کرد و بفرمود   که در تورات بنوشت معبود

2 He summoned the Jews telling them,
The Lord has written in the Torah:

۳. محمد چو ظهور آید به عالم   شما گردید بر دینش مسّلم

3 "That when Muhammad appears in the world,
You should all accept his faith, Islam."

۴. کنون از وعده چندین سال بگذشت   مسلمانتان همی باید کنون گشت

4 "Now, several years have passed since then,
All of you should now become Muslims."

۵. اگر یک یک بگویتان شهادت   همه یابید در دنیا سعادت

5 "If each and every one of you utter the *shahada*,
You shall all find happiness in this world."

۶. اگر نه همچو ملاتان همین دم   شما را میفرستم در جهنم

6 "If not, as your cleric, in an instant,
I will condemn you to Hell!"

۷. الهی هیچکس او را نبیند   درین باغ جهان این گل نچیند

7 O Lord, may no one sees such scene,
Or pick such a flower from the garden of this world.

۸. سگان استاده و ملا فتاده   شه پر قهر و سیمانطوب ستاده

8 The dogs stood tall and the cleric fell,
The king was full of rage and Simanṭov standing.[21]

۹. بترسیدند آن بیچاره ای چند   بلرزیدند چون از گرگ، گوسفند

9 They were afraid, those unlucky few,
They shook like sheep before a wolf.

۱۰. ز روی ترس، یک یک پیش رفتند   شهادت هم بدست شاه گفتند

10 Out of fear, one by one, they stepped forward,
And uttered the *shahada* in the king's presence.

21 Simantov was an earlier community leader who had been accused of theft by some members of the community and had voluntarily converted to Islam. He later had tried to save himself by reporting to the king that the Torah and other Jewish mystic books were used by the Jews as a sorcery plot against the king.

۱۱. چو یک چندی بدستِ شَه، مسلمان شدن، شُد شاه از مستی پشیمان

11 When a few had converted to Islam at the King's hands,
The king repented of his drunkenness.

۱۲. برفت خود اندرون و داد رخصت وزیر خویش را گفت او به حرمت

12 He entered his private chamber,
Speaking to his chancellor with reverence:

۱۳. هر آنکس را رئیس، مومن بیارد شهادت گوید و در دین در آرد

13 "Whomever the chief attracts to the faith
By uttering the *shahada*, becomes a believer."

۱۴. دگر چندی وزیرش داده ایمان ویک‌چندی‌سیمانطوب‌کرده‌مسلمان

14 Also some were converted to the faith by the chancellor,
And some others were converted to Islam by Simanṭov.

۱۵. نوشته جمله را یک سر اسامی بُدند هفتاد و پنج تن مرد نامی

15 Having written down all their names,
In total, the number of men was seventy-five.

۱۶. بشد روز دگر مست می ناب بگفت تورات ها ریزند در آب

16 The next day, drunk on pure wine,
The king ordered the Torahs thrown into the water.

۱۷. غلامان جمله در میدان دویدند کتاب‌ها جمله‌برسرِ پُل‌می‌کشیدند

17 The servants all ran into the city square,
Carrying the Books onto the bridge.[22]

۱۸. تمامی ریختند بر زنده رودش همه در آب شستند حرف و حروفش

18 Thrown out into *Zayandeh* River,
The words and letters were all washed away by the water.

۱۹. گرفتند رخصت ملا ابای صدیق بخاکش بسپُرند از روی تحقیق

19 Permission was obtained for the righteous Mullah Aba,
To be buried, according to custom.

۲۰. فلک این کارها را دست استاد دهد بیچارگان را زود بر باد

20 Fate has given the master the chore,
To snuff out the lives of those poor people instantly.

۲۱. چو اون بیچاره در خاکش سپردند تمامی‌گوشت‌را‌باماست‌خوردند

21 Once they buried the poor cleric,
They all ate meat with yoghurt.[23]

۲۲. مسلمانی همی کردند ناچار درِ نواب می رفتند به زنهار

22 Thus they practiced Islam against their will,
And helplessly attended the presence of the chancellor.

۲۳. بُدی شیخی به دور ان شهنشاه بهاء الدین اسم او، ترسایِ الله

23 There was a scholar living during the king's reign,
Whose name was Baha al-Din, a God-fearing man.

22 The term "bridge" refers to the bridge on Zayandehfud, in Isfahan.
23 Eating meat and dairy together is considered non-kosher and forbidden in Judaism.

۲۴. بسی حرمت بُدش در نزد شاهان　　همی‌کردند سجودش صف‌پناهان

24 He was highly revered by many kings,
And also bowed to by people of rank.

۲۵. تمامی خلق او را می ستودند　　به انگشتش به یکدیگر می نمودند

25 He was admired by all manner of people,
They pointed him out to one other.

۲۶. برفتند آن جماعت نزد آن مرد　　بگفتند شیخ، دیدی شه چه ها کرد؟

26 The Jewish community went to the scholar,
Saying, "Have you heard what the king has done?"

۲۷. بکشت ملای ما را او بناحق　　بریخت تورات را بر آب مطلق

27 "He killed our cleric unjustly,
And threw our Torahs into the running water."

۲۸. چو بشنید شیخ اینها را بر آشفت　　بزد بر سر دو دست و این چنین گفت

28 Once he heard of the news, the scholar was furious,
Pounding on his head with both hands he said:

۲۹. خداوندا من استغفار کردم　　بجای اشکِ دل، خون کار کردم

29 "O Lord, I pray for forgiveness!
Instead of tears, I shed blood."

۳۰. چنان تورات را کردند پامال　　چرا پیشش همی رفتید امسال؟

30 "How could they disrespect the Torah!
Why did you go to him at all this year?"

۳۱. کنون یک مصلحت بینم من از جان　　که شه آید مرا فردا به مهمان

31 "Now I see a solution, whole-heartedly,
Since the king will be my guest tomorrow."

۳۲. بخواهد مصلحت دیدن، ابا من　　بگوشش در برم شاید یکی فن

32 "Should he seek my opinion about the Faith,
I may present him a masterful solution."

۳۳. بپایش در فتادند و زار کردند　　سفارش هر یکی بسیار کردند

33 They fell at his feet and cried,
Each making many requests.

۳۴. از آنجا روی نهادند درگه میر　　بگفتند کرده ایمان جمله تقصیر

34 From there, they went to the chancellor's court,
Saying: "It is us all, who are at fault."

۳۵. رضای حق، بِخَر ما را دگر بار　　به درگاهت شویم روزی دو صد بار

35 "For God's sake, intercede for us, one more time,
We shall then attend your presence two hundred times a day."

۳۶. بگفتش میر محمد قاسم از کین　　بگفتم از خر شیطان به پائین[4]

36 Mir Mohammad Qasem [the chancellor] said vengefully:
"I told you not to be so stubborn!"[24]

24 As the poet reports, Mirmohamad Qasem was the name of the chancellor of Shah Abbas I's sister, who was instrumental in converting the Jews to Islam (BZI 14b: 13–14).

وزیری داشت آن همشیرهٔ شاه　　بُدی آن گُربَز و دانا و آگاه
بُدی او میرمحمّد قاسمش، نام　　برآن درگه نشسته صبح تا شام

۳۷. بیاییتان و خود ضایع مسازید ز بهر خود شش و پنج مبازید

37 "Consent and do not sow your own destruction.
For your own sake, do not gamble with your lives."

۳۸. چو نشنیدید سخن از من سرانجام همی‌نوشیدزهر اکنون‌چنان‌جام

38 "Since you did not listen to my words, as penance,
You need to drink from the cup of poison immediately."

۳۹. بگفتند دیگرش از روی زاری که‌حق‌یارت بود، چون‌حق‌گذاری

39 They responded with sorrow and moaning:
"May God be with you, since you are just."

۴۰. ز بهر حق رسان یک بارِ دیگر سلام ما به بانوی دو کشور

40 "For God's sake once again deliver,
Our salute to the lady of both lands."

۴۱. بگو یاران سلامت می رسانند که‌مارا‌چاره‌ساز، آخر ازین‌بند

41 "Tell her that her friends send their greetings,
And request a way for us out of this bind."

۴۲. صلاحی بهر این بیچارگان بین دعاگویِ‌توآند، این‌جمع‌مسکین

42 "Find a solution for us the downcast,
The poor who are all in prayer for you."

۴۳. بگفتند این و برفتند دل پر از خون زبهر دات بودند همچو مجنون

43 Having said this, they all left with bleeding hearts.
Enraged were all, for the sake of their faith.[25]

۴۴. چو یک مدت بر آمد، صحبت دین بیامد شاه نزدیکِ شیخ بهاالدین

44 After some time, the king came to visit Baha al-Din,
To discuss matters of faith with the Sheikh.

۴۵. چو شیخ معتبر شه دید از دور سجودی‌کرد واکرامی‌به‌دستور

45 When the esteemed scholar saw the king from a distance
He bowed and stood, out of respect.

۴۶. بِگفت شاها هزاران جان فدایت به‌دیده‌می‌کشم مَن خاکِ پایت

46 He said, "Your Majesty, may thousands be sacrificed for you,
May the dust under your feet be salve to my eyes."

۴۷. چگونه عذرِ مقدومت بخواهم که من یک بنده از پادشاهم

47 "How can I justify your visit to me,
For I am only a servant of your majesty?"

۴۸. بگفت شاهش که ای شیخ بصیرم مرا یک مشورت باشد به پیرم

48 The king said to him, "My wise scholar,
There is something on which I seek your advice."

۴۹. اگر سازی امیدوارم ز محشر اگر نه دست زنم بر کار دیگر

49 "I hope you can grant my wishes for Judgment Day,
If not, I will pursue another course."

۵۰. بگفت شیخش که ای خورشید خاور مرادت چیست از بازار محشر

50 The scholar answered: "O Rising Sun of the East,
What do you desire for the day of judgment?"

25 The Hebrew term "דת" (dat/دات) means "religion" in English.

۵۱. بگفت گبران ابا جمع یهودان همی خواهم کنم اینان مسلمان

51 “Zoroastrians along with the Jews,” the king replied,
“I wish to convert them all to Islam.”

۵۲. چو بشنید این سخن ها شیخ از وی بگفت هست همتت چو حاتم طَی

52 When the scholar heard his words, he replied: “Your motivation is as high as that of *Ḥatam Ṭaiee* [the benevolent].”[26]

۵۳. یهودان را نیازاری تو زنها ر که پیغمبر سفارش کرد بسیار

53 “Beware not to oppress the Jews,
Since the Prophet has strongly warned against it.”

۵۴. به تکلیف و توراتش تا توا نید یهودان را مسلمانی رسانید

54 “According to the Torah and its commands,
Honor the Jews, with the observation of Islam.”

۵۵. د گر هم خود موسایِ پیامبر ز جمع انبیا بودی کلانتر

55 “Because the Prophet Moses himself,
Was the leader of all the prophets.”

۵۶. عَشرِ آیات، او از حق گرفته به هر بابی سوی معراج رفته

56 “He received the Ten Commandments from the Lord.
He ascended through any gate, to join the Lord.”

۵۷. ولی گبران ندارند دین و ایمان به‌جوران می‌توانی کرد مسلمان

57 “But the Zoroastrians have no faith and religion,
You can convert them to Islam by force.”

۵۸. چو شه بشنید از شیخ این روایت دلش کرد از حدیث او سرایت

58 When the king heard the scholar’s view,
The king’s heart was moved by his words.

۵۹. برون آمد از آنجا شد سواره سوی نواب شد با صد لجاره

59 He went out and mounted his horse,
Setting out for the chancellor with one hundred of his men.

۶۰. بدید آنجا ستاده جمع عبری نشسته پیش ایشان میرنُخری

60 He saw a crowd of Hebrews standing there,
Sitting with them, the non-Jewish officer.

۶۱. چو شه از دور دیدند آن جماعت ابا میر آمدند در سجده ساعت

61 When the crowd saw the king from far away,
Along with the officer, they bowed down at once.

۶۲. چو شه ایشان بدید گفتا که دیگر بشد دارالیهود باز این در

62 When the king saw them, he proclaimed,
That the Jewish quarter was to be reinstated.

۶۳. فرود آمد بشد در پیش نواب به‌پایش شد روان نواب چون آب

63 Dismounted, the king approached the chancellor.
Who kneeled down in his presence, like running water.

26 Farhang-e Mo‘in: S.V. “Ḥatam Ṭaiee”: A well-known generous and benevolent individual in one of the Pre-Islamic Arab tribes.

۶۴. نشاندش بر صف و بر پاش زر ریخت   به خدمت یک زمان چون شمع آویخت

64 Having seated the king in the front row and poured gold at his feet,
In the king's service, the chancellor melted down like a candle.

۶۵. پس از خدمت، بکردند گفتگو را   به هر شهری به هر جائی سخن ها

65 After paying homage, they began to converse,
Discussing the issues of various cities and places.

۶۶. سخن اندر سخن آمد به بیرون   که تا آمد یکی حرف از یهودان

66 They spoke widely on all subjects,
Until the issue of the Jews came up.

۶۷. به منت خواست نواب عَلیهِ   که ایشان میدهند هر ماه جزیه

67 The chancellor petitioned that the Jews,
Pay their taxes to the treasury every month.

۶۸. حلال است پول ایشان ای برادر   مده ما را مواجب جای دیگر

68 "Assuming that the Jewish tax is religiously acceptable,
Your monthly payment of salary to us is not needed."

۶۹. نهاد او منّتی بر دوش آن ماه   که بخشیدم بتو این قوم گمراه

69 The king accepted the request of his chancellor,
Saying "I grant you these ignorant people."

۷۰. الهی حرف نابی را بیان کن   گئولاه را به بابائی عیان کن

70 O Lord, please deliver the promise of our prophet,
And reveal redemption to Baba'i.

Lyric Poetry

אשעאר מרבות בה זיבאיי ו טביעת
اشعار مربوط به زیبایی و طبیعت
Poetry on Beauty of the Nature[27]

1. ש'דה בוסתאן בהשת ו חוץ' כוות'ר   גֶמנגאהי זבאג' כ''לד בהתר
2. ש'דה אזסבזהכ''ררםדשתוכוהסאר   בהאראן בוד וצחרא גֶון ר'ך' יאר
3. ריאחין תאגֹ זר בנהאדה בר סר   גֶמן רכ'ת זמרד כדדה דר בר
4. סר אנדר פאי יך דיגר נהאדה   דרכ'תאן גֶו ערוסאן רך' גשאדה
5. גרפ'תש סרו' אנדר בר גֶו דאיה   פ'כנדה פ'אכ'תה בר סרו' סאיה
6. קבאהאי ג''נגֶה רא דר בר דרידי   צבא הר לחט'ה דר בוסתאן דוידי
7. גהי ח'סן ריאחין אב דאדי   גהי זלף' בנפ'שה תאב דאדי
8. גהי ברכ'אסתי גאהי נשסתי   דו'ידי הר טרף' מאננד מסתי

27 'Emrāni, *Fatḥnāmeh*, ms. BZI 964 ff. 21b:16–21a:9.

9. גהי גִעד גֶמן רא דאנה כרדי   גהי ארג'ו'אן סומב'ל שאנה כרדי
10. זמאני סר בפאיה ג'ל נהאדי   זמאני ג''נגֶה רא דל באז דאדי
11. גרפ'תה לאלה גִאם ארג'ו'אני   נהאדה ג'ל סריר כ''סרואני
12. ז ז'אלה צד קדח דר דסת לאלה   נהאדה נרגס אנדר כף' פיאלה
13. גֶמן גרדיד צורת כ'אנה גֶין   זשכל סבזה ו חסן ריאחין
14. בנפ'שה זלף רא בגשאדה אז תאב   פ'כנדה סרו' סאיה בר לב אב
15. גרפ'תה ארג'ו'אן גִאם מיי צאף   זבאן בגשאד סוסן בהר אווסף
16. שדה נילופ'ר אנדר באג' חאגִב   שקאיק גשתה בא כ'יירי מצאחב
17. נדאדה ברג בידש، ראה כ'ורשיד   צנובר כרדה סאיה בר סר ביד
18. גֶראן בא הם גו'זן ו גור ו אהו   דר או'אז אמדה מ'רג'אן בה הר סו
19. רו'אן גרדידה גרד באג' ו בוסתאן   בה הר סו גֶשמהאי גֶון אב חייואן

۱. چمنگاهی ز باغ خُلد بهتر   شده‌بوستان، بهشت‌وحوضِ‌کوثر

1 A meadow more pleasant than Eden,
Or Paradise, with the spring of Kowsar.

۲. بهاران بود وصحرا چون رخ یار   شده‌ازسبزه‌خرم‌دشت‌وکوهسار

2 Spring has arrived and, like the face of the beloved friend,
All the land, from the deserts to the mountains, is cheerful and green.

۳. چمن رخت زمرد کرده در بر   ریاحین تاج زر بنهاده بر سر

3 Meadows have donned emerald dresses,
Sweet basils wear a golden crown.

۴. درختان چوعروسان رُخ گشاده   سر اندر پای یک دیگر نهاده

4 The trees have blossomed like brides' faces,
Embracing one another gracefully.

۵. فکنده فاخته بر سرو سایه   گرفتش سرو اندر بر چو دایه

5 The ringdove casts its shadow on the cypress,
The cypress draws him in, like a mother to a child.

۶. صبا هر لحظه دربوستان دویدی   قباهای غنچه را در بردریدی

6 Zephyr never ceases to blow in the garden,
Tearing the cloaks off the buds.

۷. گهی زلف بنفشه تاب دادی   گهی حسن ریاحین آب دادی

7 Sometimes he brushes the violet's curls,
Sometimes leaving dew on the sweet basil.

۸. دویدی هر طرف مانند مستی   گهی برخاستی گاهی نشستی

8 Zephyr blows in all directions, like a drunkard.
Sometimes he rises, and sometimes he recedes.

۹. گهی ارغوان سمبل شانه کردی   گهی جعد چمن را دانه کردی

9 Sometimes the Judas tree brushes hyacinths' curls,
Sometimes he combs through the tresses of the grass.

۱۰. زمانی غنچه را دل باز دادی   زمانی سر به پای گل نهادی

10 For a time, the rose bud would open up and bloom,
At other times, it would bow down to the rose.

نهاده گل سریر خسروانی   گرفته لاله، جام ارغوانی ۱۱.
11 The rose has the posture of a king,
Whereas the tulip is shaped like a crimson chalice.

نهاده نرگس اندر کف پیاله   ز ژاله صد قدح در دست لاله ۱۲.
12 While the narcissus clasps a goblet of wine in her hand,
The tulip holds a hundred cups of dew.

ز شکل سبزه و حسن ریاحین   چمن گردید صورتخانهِ چین ۱۳.
13 The green of the grass and the sweet perfume of herbs,
Has made the meadow resemble a Chinese art studio.

فکنده سرو سایه بر لب آب   بنفشه زلف را بگشاده از تاب ۱۴.
14 The cypress casts a shadow on the water's edge,
The violet has uncurled the twist of her locks.

زبان بگشاد سوسن بهر اوصاف   گرفته ارغوان جامِ مِیِ صاف ۱۵.
15 The lily blooms for the sake of showing her beauty,
Just as the Judas tree holds a red goblet of pure wine.

شقایق گشته با خیری مصاحب   شده نیلوفر اندر باغ حاجب ۱۶.
16 The poppy and the marigold enjoy each other's company,
And the morning glory has become the garden's master of ceremonies.

صنوبر کرده سایه بر سر بید   نداده برگ بیدش، راه خورشید
17 The pine casts such a shadow upon the willow that, ۱۷.
The sun's rays cannot shine through the willow's leaves.

در آواز آمده مرغان به هر سو   چران با هم گوزن و گور و آهو
18 In any direction, the birds have started to sing, ۱۸.
While stags, zebras and gazelles graze together.

به هرسو چشمه ای چون آب حیوان   روان گردیده گِرد باغ وبوستان
19 Everywhere there is a spring like the fountain of life, ۱۹.
Flowing through the garden and its greenery.

סאקינאמה
ساقی نامه
Saqināmeh[28]

1. די מרא כ'אנד פיר מייכ'אנה   גפ'ת כאיי ניך בכ'ת פ'רזאנה
2. פ'צל נוורוז ו נוו בהאר אמד   כאר כ'ן האן כה וקת כאר אמד
3. בלבלאן דר סמאע נוורוזי   גֶנד באשי תו דר ג'ם רוזי
4. באדהצאף'והר'איגאןבכ'שאסת   בבר אז באדה בכ'ש תא נקש אסת
5. בכ'ש תו נקש יאר כ'ואהד בוד   באש אז בכ'ש ו נקש כ'ויש כ'ושנוד
6. בבר אז יאר ו באדה בכ'שי גֶנד   כ'וש בגו כ'וש בגוי נקשי גֶנד
7. סאקי אן באדה רא ביאר ביאר   תא שו'ם אז נשאט בר כ'ורדאר
8. מטרב אן פרדה [רא] בסאז בסאז   בר כש איי יאר באזבין או'אז

28 Netzer, "Adabiyat-e Yahud-e Iran", pt. 1, pp. 99–106: by 'Emrāni.

9. ג'ם רוזי מכ'ור כה רוזי דה   מידהד רוזי אז יכי תא דה
10. בר סר מנבר דרכ'ת ג'ל   ו'עט' מיגפ'ת צבחגה ב'לב'ל
11. דוסתאן ו'קת בוסתאן אמד   ו'קת שאדי דוסתאן אמד
12. באדה דר כאסהי בלור כניד   מדעי רא דו גֶשם כור כניד
13. מיי בנושיד ו ג'ל בר אפ'שאניד   דאד שאדי ו עייש בסתאניד
14. אפ'רין כ''דא בדאן דל באד   כה זבנד גִהאן בו'ד אזאד
15. 'ק'מרי ו'קת צבח בר סר סרו   שרח מי כרד ראז דל בה תד'רו
16. צחבת באג' רא ג'נימת דאן   סאיהי ביד ו פאי אב רו'אן
17. כ'ושבגוכ'ושבכ'נדוכ'רםבאש   שאדמאני ג'זין ו בי ג'ם באש
18. בר גִהאן גֶון בקאי גֶנדאן ניסת   כ'ושתראזבאג'וראג'ואייו'אניסת
19. מטרבי דוש פיש פיר מג'אן   גֶנג מיזד בה פיש מג'בגֶאן
20. המדמאני כה פיש אזין בודנד   כ'אך גשתנד ו באד פיימוודנד

۱. دی مرا خواند پیر میخانه   گفت کای نیک بخت فرزانه

1 Last night, the tavern sage called me,
Saying "Oh you, the fortunate and wise!"

۲. فصل نوروز و نو بهار آمد   کار کن هان که وقت کار آمد

2 "The season of Nowruz and Springtime has arrived,
Work, for the time for work has arrived."

۳. بلبلان در سماع نوروزی   چند باشی تو در غم روزی

3 "The nightingales are singing the melodies of Nowruz.
For how long must you worry about your daily bread?"

۴. باده صاف و هوای جان بخش است   ببر از باده بخش تا نقش است

4 "The wine is pure and clear, and the air life-giving,
As long as you have a trace of life, take advantage of the wine."

۵. بخش تو نقش یار خواهد بود   باش از بخش ونقش خویش خوشنود

5 "Reflect upon the beloved in your life,
Be happy for your lot, your share and your role."

۶. ببر از یار و باده بخشی چند   خوش بگو خوش بجوی نقشی چند

6 "Take your share of pleasure from the wine and beloved,
Speak joyously, and take pleasure in seeking the truth."

۷. ساقی آن باده را بیار بیار   تا شوم از نشاط بر خوردار

7 "Oh cupbearer, bring the wine, bring it,
So that I may be fulfilled by joy!"

۸. مطرب آن پرده را بساز بساز   بر کش ای یار نازنین آواز

8 "Musicians, play that music, play it!
And you, beloved, begin to sing."

۹. غم روزی مخور که روزی ده   میدهد روزی از یکی تا ده

9 "Do not worry about the daily bread, because the breadwinner,
Will provide you with one to ten loaves."

۱۰. بر سر منبر درخت گل   وعظ می گفت صبحگه بلبل

10 As if on a pulpit, sitting on a flowering tree,
The nightingale was preaching at dawn.

دوستان وقت بوستان آمد وقت شادیِ دوستان آمد
11 Oh friends, it is time to arrive in the garden, .۱۱
The time of joy and happiness is upon us.

باده در کاسهٔ بلور کنید مدعی را دو چشم کور کنید
12 Pour the wine in crystal cup, .۱۲
Make the opponent's both eyes blind.

می بنوشید و گل برافشانید داد شادی و عیش بستانید
13 Drink wine and scatter roses, .۱۳
Shout for happiness and joy.

آفرین خدا بدان دل با د که ز بند جهان بود آزاد
14 God bless that heart, .۱۴
Which will soon be free of this world.

قمری وقت صبح بر سر سرو شرح می کرد راز دل به تذرو
15 The turtledove, from the top of the cypress, .۱۵
Was explaining the mysteries of the heart to the pheasant.

صحبت باغ را غنیمت دان سایهٔ بید و پای آب روان
16 Take advantage of what you hear in the garden, .۱۶
From the shade of the willow, and the water that flows there too.

خوش بگو خوش بخند وخرّم باش شادمانی گزین و بی غم باش
17 Say good words, laugh well, and be happy, .۱۷
Choose to be joyful and prevent sadness.

بر جهان چون بقای چندان نیست خوشتر از باغ وراغ وایوان نیست
18 Since nothing in this world is eternal, .۱۸
Nothing is more pleasant than the garden, meadow and verandas.

مطربی دوش پیش پیر مغان چنگ می زد به پیش مغبچگان
19 Last night a musician, before Magi, .۱۹
And the sons of Magi, played his lute.

همدمانی که پیش ازین بودند خاک گشتند و با د پیمودند
20 Those who were your partners before, .۲۰
All left and became dust, scattered to the wind.

באמיד ו'צאל מהרת
بامید وصال مهرت
In the Hope of Uniting with Your Love[29]

1. בה א'מיד ו'צאל מהרת איי דוסת נהאדם דאג' הגְראן דר רג ו פוסת
2. בה תא כיי כ'ון כ"ורם אז טען דשמן כ'לאצי דה מרא זין דאג' גְאן סוז
3. גיולאה ב'רד אגר צבר ו קרארם א'מידם גֶון תויי היץְ ג'ם נדארם
4. כרם פ'רמא אסיראן רא חמאית אלאהי תו רסאני בר דיארם

۱. به امید وصال مهرت ای دوست نهادم داغ هجران دررگ و پوست
1 In the hope of uniting with your love, my beloved,
I marked my veins and skin with scars of separation.

29 Netzer, *Montakhab*, p. 50: two couplets, by Yousef Ben Esḥāq Yahudi.

۲. به تا کی‌خون خورم از طعن دشمن   خلاصی ده‌مرا زین داغ جانسوز

2 How long must I suffer from my enemy's scorn,
Release me from my soul's burning pain.

۳. گئولاهه برد اگر صبر و قرارم   امیدم چون تویی هیچ غم ندارم

3 In waiting for salvation, if my patience and tolerance are gone,
I will not worry as you are my hope.

۴. کرم فرما اسیران را حمایت   الهی تو رسانی بر دیارم

4 Be merciful and protect us captives,
Oh God, take me back to my land.[30]

אשער עאשקאנה
اشعار عاشقانه
Romantic Couplets[31]

1. פס וקתי כה שאה גשתי מסת   סוי אן דר ש'די כליד בה דסת
2. דר ג'שאדי ודר ש'די בה בהשת   דידי אן נקשהאי כ'וב סרשת
3. מאנדה גון תשנהאי בראבר אב   בה תמנאי אן שדי דר כ'ואב
4. מהר אן דכ'תראן חור סרשת   דר דלש ת'כ'ם מהרבאני כשת
5. גו גירם כ'אמה דר כפ'גאה אן שאה   פדיד ארם נקשי נג'ז ו גויא
6. כ'טי זיבא תר אז כ'ט גר'אנאן   כ'טי פ'ר חלקהתר אז זלף' כ'ובאן
7. ביא אז כ'ט כ'וש סטרי רקם דאן   רקם אז נכתה נוך קלם דאן
8. כה כ'טש מאיה גאו'יד באשד   סראפא אית אמיד באשד

۱. پس وقتی که شاه گشتی مست   سوی آن در شدی کلید به دست

1 Thus, when the king got drunk
He approached the gate key in hand

۲. در گشادی و در شدی به بهشت   دیدی آن نقش های خوب سرشت

2 He opened the gate and stepped into Paradise,
And saw the portraits of beauty there.

۳. مانده چون تشنه ای برابر آب   به تمنای آن شدی در خواب

3 He stood like a thirsty man by fresh water,
Filled with longing, as though in a dream.

۴. مهر آن دختران حور سرشت   دردلش تخم مهربانی کشت

4 The passion he felt for those girls in the garden,
Sowed the seeds of love in his heart.

۵. گو گیرم خامه در کف گاه آن شاه   پدید آرم نقشی نغز و گویا

5 "I will take a paintbrush and pen," so he said,
"And paint fetching forms, forms that will speak.

30 Netzer, "Adabiyat-e Yahud-e Iran", pt. 1, p. 73, the term "land" here is a reference to "my homeland, Israel".

31 Four Doors displayed at the Light and Shadow Conference, Tel Aviv University, 2010, UCLA 2012.

۶. خطی زیبا تر از خط جوانان   خطی پر حلقه‌تر از زلف خوبان

6 “With faces more ravishing than those of these girls,
And lovelier curls than the tresses they have.”

۷. بیا از خط خوش سطری رقم دان   رقم از نکته نوک قلم دان

7 Come if you please with brush and with quill,
And paint lines and faces if only you will.

۸. که خطش مایه جاوید باشد   سراپا آیت امید باشد

8 Because a fine painting will last for all time,
And that will be a sign of hope wherever you go.

Vernacular Poetry

שיראי חאתאני
شیرای حاتانی
Wedding Song[32]

1. ש'די חאתאן מ'בארך באד   השם פ'שת ו פנאהת באד
2. טו'יל ע'מרי המראהת באד   בה ניך נאמי דר איסראיל

שלך' גואל שלך' גואל
זכ'ות נאבי יקותיאל

4. ש'די דאמאד מ'בארך באד   סר ו גִאנם פ'דאית באד
5. כ''דא פ'שת ו פנאהת באד   עלם גרדי בה איסראיל

שלך' גואל שלך' גואל
זכ'ות נאבי יקותיאל

7. הזאראן ש'כר ש'די דאמאד   חקיר בסיאר ש'דם דלשאד
8. זנוו שירא כ'נים ב'ניאד   המה ו'צף' נאבי הא אל

שלך' גואל שלך' גואל
זכ'ות נאבי יקותיאל

10. הזאראן ש'כר ש'די בר פא   רסידי תו' בר חופא
11. ניופ'תי איי גִו'אן אז פ'א   עלם גרדי בה איסראיל

שלך' גואל שלך' גואל
זכ'ות נאבי יקותיאל

13. בדוזיד רכ'ת דאמאדי   אלאהי ח'כם כ'וד דאדי
14. בבנדיד חגִלהי שאדי   כ'ושא בר קום איסראיל

שלך' גואל שלך' גואל
זכ'ות נאבי יקותיאל

16. ו'גִודת כם מבאד חאתאן   ניאיד נזד תו סאטאן
17. תויי חאו'ר גֶ'ו יהונאתאן   כה בא דאו'וד ב'דנד כ'ושדל

שלך'גואל שלך' גואל
זכ'ות נאבי יקותיאל

19 קדת סרו' ו ר'כ'ת ג'לשן   גֶראג' דאימת רוושן
20 בה בן זאכ'אר שוי כ''רסנד   זכ'ות נאבי שמואל

שלך' גואל שלך' גואל
זכ'ות נאבי יקותיאל

32 Netzer, "Adabiyat-e Yahud-e Iran", pt. 1, pp. 107/114. For a detailed article, see Sarah Soroudi. 1982. Shirā-ye Hatani, A Judeo-Persian Wedding Song. *Irano-Judaica*, vol. 1. Jerusalem: Ben Zvi Institute. pp. 204–264.

22. אקא חאתאן שו'י קייאם — זחק דאים בגירי כאם
23. כה מת'לת ניסת דר אין איאם — בביני גֶהרהי גואל
שלך' גואל שלך' גואל
זכ'ות נאבי יקותיאל
25. תויי באחור בראזנדה — בה גֶשם כ'לק כ'וש אינדה
26. דר אין עאלם תו פאינדה — בה דוורת איד אן גואל
שלך' גואל שלך' גואל
זכ'ות נאבי יקותיאל
28. תורא דידם פסנדידם — ש'דם כ'ושחאל ו כ'נדידם
29. סראפ'ראזי זתוו דידם — מייאן גִמע איסראיל
שלך' גואל שלך' גואל
זכ'ות נאבי יקותיאל
31. קדת גֶון סרו' אזאד אסת — ר'כ'ת גֶון מה כ''דאדאד אסת
32. גֶו יוסף' שאך' שמשאד אסת — שוי גִבכאר דר איסראיל
שלך' גואל שלך' גואל
זכ'ות נאבי יקותיאל
34. נגרדאנם זאמרת סר — המה פ'רמאן תו בר סר
35. בבינד כ'יר תו המסר — מיאן קום איסראיל
שלך' גואל שלך' גואל
זכ'ות נאבי יקותיאל
37. איא חאתאן תויי קאבל — א'מיד האית שו'ד חאצל
38. דר איאמת שו'נד ואצל — מיאן גִמע איסראיל
שלך' גואל שלך' גואל
זכ'ות נאבי יקותיאל
40. אקא חאתאן קום מ'שה — כ''דא בכ'שד בה תו רישה
41. אז אן רישה דו צד כ'ושה — עלם גרדי בה איסראיל
שלך' גואל שלך' גואל
זכ'ות נאבי יקותיאל
43. כ''דא באשד נגהדארת — דהד פירוזי דר כארת
44. ב'ו'ד מאדאם סאלארת — ו' הם בר קום איסראיל
שלך' גואל שלך' גואל
זכ'ות נאבי יקותיאל
46. בה סימאנטוב ש'די חאתאן — שו'ד יא רב תורא ס'לטאן
47. שו'י ג'אלב תו בר סאטאן — קו'י בר דין איסראיל
שלך' גואל שלך' גואל
זכ'ות נאבי יקותיאל
49. כ''דא באשד נציר תו — בה המראה ו ו'זיר תו
50. שו'ד דוולת אסיר תו — שו'י נאמדאר דר איסראיל
שלך' גואל שלך' גואל
זכ'ות נאבי יקותיאל
52 ערוסת כאם דארת באד — שו'ד אז ג'ם דלת אזאד
53 כ'נד כאשאנה את אבאד — בה ניך נאמי דר איסראיל
שלך' גואל שלך' גואל
זכ'ות נאבי יקותיאל

55. אקא "חאתאן" נגִיב זאדה　　כ"דא תאגִי בה סר דאדה
56. גֶו אין "כללאה" בה תו דאדה　　שו'יד פיר ו בהם כ'ושדל
שלך' גואל שלך' גואל
זכ'ות נאבי יקותיאל
58. בה פאי הם שו'יד דלשאד　　בגיריד כאם ו הם ב'ניאד
59. כה ציון הם שו'ד אבאד　　דר או גירים המה מנזל
שלך' גואל שלך' גואל
זכ'ות נאבי יקותיאל
61. המה יאראן ו ג'מכ'וארן　　עלמדאראן ו סרדאראן
62. בה בזם אייד ס'רוד כ'ואנאן　　בראי קוום איסראיל
שלך' גואל שלך' גואל
זכ'ות נאבי יקותיאל
64. דר אין הפ'ת רוז כה תו שאהי　　ו הם ס'לטאן ו אקאיי
65. הר אן כ'דמת כה פ'רמאיי　　בגִא ארים בגִאן ו דל
שלך' גואל שלך' גואל
זכ'ות נאבי יקותיאל
67. דר אין הפ'ת רוז תו אזאדי　　בה בזם ו עייש בפרדאזי
68. ולי כ'וד רא ביאנדאזי　　ז רסם דין איסראיל
שלך' גואל שלך' גואל
זכ'ות נאבי יקותיאל
70. זח'כם אדר יכתא　　כה תא יך סאל תו בא המתא
71. שו'יד משג'ול בר עייש　　תא בביניד כ'יר דר איסראיל
שלך' גואל שלך' גואל
זכ'ות נאבי יקותיאל
73. בשוו כ'ושנוד בה המזאדת　　נציבת אין כ"דא דאדת
74. תורא המראה פ'רסתאדת　　המאן ס'לטאן איסראיל
שלך' גואל שלך' גואל
זכ'ות נאבי יקותיאל
76. עלמו'ארי ב'לנדם כ'ן　　אגר זשתם פסנדם כ'ן
77. אגר תלכ'ם גֶו קנדם כון　　מיאן גִמע איסראיל
שלך' גואל שלך'גואל
זכ'ות נאבי יקותיאל
79. השם באשד בה תו יאו'ר　　שו'נד כ'שנוד פדר מאדר
80. מ'דאם באשי סרו סרו'ר　　מיאן גִמע איסראיל
שלך' גואל שלך' גואל
זכ'ות נאבי יקותיאל
82. השם באשד אבא תו יאר　　בגרדד נסל תו בסיאר
83. זכ'ות פינחאס אלעאזאר　　כה אוסת מאג'ן בה איסראיל
שלך' גואל שלך'גואל
זכ'ות נאבי יקותיאל
85 כללא" כ'אנ'ם רכ'ש גלזאר　　פ'רי בטנש המה פ'ר דאר"
86 כה ארד פור מת'אל נאר　　דו'אזדה פור המה יך דל
שלך' גואל שלך' גואל
זכ'ות נאבי יקותיאל

88. בבכ'שאיד בה תו דאו'ר   דו'אזדה פור נאם או'ר
89. תרא חק יאר ו הם יאו'ר   עלם גרדי בה איסראיל
שלך' גואל שלך' גואל
זכ'ות נאבי יקותיאל
91. שו'ד עמרת גְו בן עמראן   שו'י דלשאד ז פ'רזנדאן
92. גְו יעקוב נבי פר דאן   בה כאם דל דר איסראיל
שלך' גואל שלך' גואל
זכ'ות נאבי יקותיאל
94. נדא אמד כה יא מוסי   בגיר דר דסת תו אין עצא
95. ברו דר מצר בכן נס הא   בראי קום איסראיל
שלך' גואל שלך' גואל
זכ'ות נאבי יקותיאל
97. רסיד מוסי לב דריא   בדיד דשמן קפ'א נאגאה
98. בזד נאלה בגפ'ת אללה   אז אין דריא בדה גואל
שלך' גואל שלך' גואל
זכ'ות נאבי יקותיאל
100. נדא אמד כה אי מוסי   גְה ו'קת נאלה אסת אינגְא
101. בגיר דר דסת המאן עצא   דר אין דריא מנם גואל
שלך' גואל שלך' גואל
זכ'ות נאבי יקותיאל
103. נבי בשניד ו ש'ד כ'שנוד   עצא בר דסת בש'ד בר רוד
104. בה דה גְאדה כה חק פ'רמוד   כה תא ד'שמן שו'ד נופ'ל
שלך' גואל שלך' גואל
זכ'ות נאבי יקותיאל
106. גְה גוים וצפ' בן עמראם   גזין כ'ואהר גְנאן מיריאם
107. ברון או'רדמאן זאן יאם   שירא גפ'תנד בראי אל
שלך' גואל שלך' גואל
זכ'ות נאבי יקותיאל
109. שו'ד אבאד בית המיקדאש   חכ'אמים הא כ'נבד דראאש
110. ס'ד תוראה בגרדד פ'אש   "מקבץ נידחה" איסראיל
שלך' גואל שלך' גואל
זכ'ות נאבי יקותיאל
112. המה אנהא כה דר כ'ואבנד   שו'נד בידאר ו דריאבנד
113. ז נור חק המי תאבנד   כה מאיים קום איסראיל
שלך' גואל שלך' גואל
זכ'ות נאבי יקותיאל
115 ז תו יכתא המי כ'ואהים   דוסת ו דשמן כ'ני אז הם
116 סוי מיקדאש רו'ים בא הם   כ'הן לו'י ו איסראיל
שלך' גואל שלך' גואל
זכ'ות נאבי יקותיאל

118. המה הסתים בה אין אמיד   בבינים רוי בן דאו'יד

119. אמיד מא נש'ד נוומיד   איד גויל בה איסראיל

שלך' גואל שלך'גואל

זכ'ות נאבי יקותיאל

121. גאולאה רא ט'אהר גרדאן   מכן מא רא תו סרגרדאן

122. דשמן הא רא תו ניסת גרדאן   רסאן מא רא בה איסראיל

שלך' גואל שלך' גואל

זכ'ות נאבי יקותיאל

124. פ'רסת בר מא גאולאה רא   בבכ'ש בר מא ישועא רא

125. בבר בר שהר כ'וד מא רא   כה תא גירים דר או מנזל

שלך' גואל שלך' גואל

זכ'ות נאבי יקותיאל

127. כ'דאי קאדר סבחאן   מאשיח רא במא ברסאן

128. אז אין גאלותמאן ברהאן   זנד שופ'אר זרובאבל

שלך' גואל שלך' גואל

זכ'ות נאבי יקותיאל

130. אגר מא כ'וד גנה כארים   שפ'אעת כ'ואה בסי דארים

131. גֶו מוסי פיר חק דארים   נמי תרסים ז היץֶ עארל

שלך' גואל שלך' גואל

זכ'ות נאבי יקותיאל

133. דר אן איאם כה או איד   דר רחמת גֶו בגשאיד

134. דיגר גאלות נפ'ר מאיד   כסי בר קום איסראיל

שלך' גואל שלך' גואל

זכ'ות נאבי יקותיאל

136. מאשיח סוי מא איד   גאולא תא אבד פאיד

137. שו'ד האדי ו בנמאיד   רה תחקיק בהר שואֶל

שלך' גואל שלך' גואל

זכ'ות נאבי יקותיאל

139. בית המיקדאש שו'ד אבאד   אזין גאלות שו'ים אזאד

140. רו'ים כ'אנה שו'ים דלשאד   ז נור כ'אץ איסראיל

שלך' גואל שלך' גואל

זכ'ות נאבי יקותיאל

142. המה איים בה דלכ'ואהי   בה דו גֶשמאן בינאיי

143. דר הכ'אל בגשאיי   בראי קוום איסראיל

שלך' גואל שלך' גואל

זכ'ות נאבי יקותיאל

145. תוראה מא בו'ד כאמל   שמא איי מלת עאקל

146. רה סאטאן כניד באטל   כ'ושא בר קוום איסראיל

שלך' גואל שלך' גואל

זכ'ות נאבי יקותיאל

148. אקא חאתאן מ'בארך באד השם פ'שת ו פנאהת באד
149. ערוסת שאד ו כ'רם באד בה ניך נאמי דר איסראיל
שלך' גואל שלך' גואל
זכ'ות נאבי יקותיאל

۱. شدی حاتان مبارک باد هَشِم پشت و پناهت باد

1 You became a groom, be blessed,
May the Lord be with you and protect you.

۲. طویل عمری همراهت باد به نیک نامی در ایسرایل

2 May long life be your companion,
With an honorable name among the [people] of Israel.[33]

شلح گوئل، شلح گوئل، زخوت نابی یقوتیئل

Send us redemption, Send us redemption,
In the merit of our prophet, Yeghutiel.[34]

۴. شدی داماد مبارک باد سر و جانم فدایت باد

4 You became a groom, be blessed,
May my body and soul be sacrificed for you.

۵. خدا پشت و پناهت باد عَلَم گردی به ایسرایل

5 May the Lord be with you and protect you,
May you be exalted amongst the [people]of Israel.

شلح گوئل، شلح گوئل، زخوت نابی یقوتیئل

Send us redemption, Send us redemption,
In the merit of our prophet, Yeghutiel.

۷. هزاران شکر، شدی داماد حقیر بسیار شدم دلشاد

7 A thousand praises, for your becoming a groom,
This humble one is very happy at heart.

۸. ز نو شیرا کنیم بنیاد همه وصف نابی ها اِل

8 Let's start singing all over again,
In praise of the messenger of the Lord.[35]

شلح گوئل، شلح گوئل، زخوت نابی یقوتیئل

Send us redemption, Send us redemption,
In the merit of our prophet, Yeghutiel.

۱۰. هزاران شکر شدی برپا رسیدی تو برِ خوپا

10 A thousand praises for you becoming a groom,
That you have arrived at the bridal canopy.

33 "Israel" is another name for Jacob.

34 "Yeghutiel" is another name for Moses. The Hebrew term "זכ'ות" (Zekhut/ زخوت) means "merit".

35 The Hebrew term "הא אל" (ha El/ ها اِل) is a reference to the Lord.

۱۱. نیفتی ای جوان از پا علَم گردی به ایسرایل

11 Young man, may you never fall down,
May you be exalted amongst the [people] of Israelite.

شلح گوئل، شلح گوئل، زخوت نابی یقوتیئل

Send us redemption, Send us redemption,
In the merit of our prophet, Yeghutiel.

۱۳. بدوزید رخت دامادی الهی حکم خود دادی

13 Sew clothes for the groom,
Lord you have given your command.

۱۴. ببندید حجلهٔ شادی خوشا بر قوم ایسرایل

14 Build a bridal chamber of joy,
How joyous for the people of Israel.

شلح گوئل، شلح گوئل، زخوت نابی یقوتیئل

Send us redemption, Send us redemption,
In the merit of our prophet, Yeghutiel.

۱۶. وجودت کم مباد حاتان نیاید نزد تو ساطان

16 O groom, may you never lack anything,
May the devil never approach you.

۱۷. تویی حاور چو یهوناتان که با داوود بُدند خوشدل

17 You are a friend like Jonathan,
With whom David was joyous.

شلح گوئل، شلح گوئل، زخوت نابی یقوتیئل

Send us redemption, Send us redemption,
In the merit of our prophet, Yeghutiel.

۱۹.
قدت سرو و رُخت گلشن چراغ دایمت روشن

19 You are tall like a cypress tree, with a flower like face,
May your light shine eternally.

۲۰. به بن زاخار شوی خرسند زخوت نابی شموئل

20 May you be granted a male son,
In the merit of the prophet, Samuel.[36]

شلح گوئل، شلح گوئل، زخوت نابی یقوتیئل

Send us redemption, Send us redemption,
In the merit of our prophet, Yeghutiel.

۲۲. آقا حاتان شوی قَیام ز حقّ، دایم بگیری کام

22 Master groom, may you be strong,
May you get constant serenity from the Lord.

۲۳. که مثالت نیست در این ایام ببینی چهره گوئل

23 So peerless are you at this time,
May you see the face of the Redeemer.

شلح گوئل، شلح گوئل، زخوت نابی یقوتیئل

Send us redemption, Send us redemption,
In the merit of our prophet, Yeghutiel.

36 The Hebrew term "בן זאכ'אר" (ben zakhor/بن زاخور) means "first-born son" in English.

۲۵. تویی با حور برازنده به چشم خلق خوش آینده

25 You are worthy to be with a heavenly angel,
Well wished, in the eyes of the people.

۲۶. در این عالم تو پاینده به دورت آید آن گویل

26 In this world you are eternal,
May the Redeemer surround you.

شلح گوئل، شلح گوئل، زخوت نابی یقوتیئل

Send us redemption, Send us redemption,
In the merit of our prophet, Yeghutiel.

۲۸. ترا دیدم پسندیدم شدم خوشحال و خندیدم

28 I saw you and found you suitable,
I became joyous and I smiled.

۲۹. سرافرازی ز تو دیدم میان جمع ایسرایل

29 I have seen honor in you,
Amidst all the people of Israel.

شلح گوئل، شلح گوئل، زخوت نابی یقوتیئل

Send us redemption, Send us redemption,
In the merit of our prophet, Yeghutiel.

۳۱. قدت چون سرو آزاد است رُخت چون مه خداداد است

31 You are tall, as a liberated cypress tree,
Your face is God-given, like the moon.

۳۲. چو یوسف شاخ شمشاد است شوی جبّار در ایسرایل

32 Like Joseph you are as slim as a box tree,
May you be powerful amongst the [people] of Israel.

شلح گوئل، شلح گوئل، زخوت نابی یقوتیئل

Send us redemption, Send us redemption,
In the merit of our prophet, Yeghutiel.

۳۴. نگردانم ز امرت سر همه فرمان تو بر سر

34 I will never turn down your orders,
Everyone will follow your lead.

۳۵. ببیند خیر تو همسر میان قوم ایسرایل

35 May your spouse be blessed because of you,
Amongst the people of Israel.

شلح گوئل، شلح گوئل، زخوت نابی یقوتیئل

Send us redemption, Send us redemption,
In the merit of our prophet, Yeghutiel.

۳۷. ایا حاتان تویی قابل امیدهایت شود حاصل

37 O groom, you are worthy,
May your wishes all come true.

۳۸. در ایامت شوند واصل میانِ جمعِ ایسرایل

38 In your time may they [the redeemers] arrive,
Amongst the community of Israel

شلح گوئل، شلح گوئل، زخوت ناوی یقوتیئل

Send us redemption, Send us redemption,
In the merit of our prophet, Yeghutiel.

۴۰. آقا حاتان، قومِ موشه   خدا بخشد بتو ریشه

40 Oh groom, man from the nation of Moses,
May God grant you roots.

۴۱. از آن ریشه دو صد خوشه   علم گردی به ایسرایل

41 May your roots branch out to hundreds,
May you rise amongst the [people] of Israel.

شلح گوئل، شلح گوئل، زخوت نابی یقوتیئل

Send us redemption, Send us redemption,
In the merit of our prophet, Yeghutiel.

۴۳. خدا باشد نگهدارت   دهد پیروزی در کارت

43 May the Lord be your protector,
May He make you victorious in your profession.

۴۴. بُوَد مادام سالارت   و هم بر قوم ایسرایل

44 May He always be your Lord,
And also for the people of Israel.

شلح گوئل، شلح گوئل، زخوت نابی یقوتیئل

Send us redemption, Send us redemption,
In the merit of our prophet, Yeghutiel.

۴۶. به سیمانطوب شدی حاتان   شود یارب ترا سلطان

46 With good fortune you have become a groom,
May the Lord be your king.

۴۷. شوی غالب تو بر ساطان   قوی بر دین ایسرایل

47 May you prevail against the devil,
Strong in Jewish faith.

شلح گوئل، شلح گوئل، زخوت نابی یقوتیئل

Send us redemption, Send us redemption,
In the merit of our prophet, Yeghutiel.

۴۹. خدا باشد نصیر تو   به همراه و وزیر تو

49 May the Lord be your supporter,
May He be your partner and minister.

۵۰. شود دولت اسیر تو   شوی نامدار در ایسرایل

50 May fortune become your slave,
May you become famous amongst the [people] of Israel.

شلح گوئل، شلح گوئل، زخوت نابی یقوتیئل

Send us redemption, Send us redemption,
In the merit of our prophet, Yeghutiel.

۵۲. عروست کام دارت باد   شود از غم دلت آزاد

52 May your bride bring you serenity,
May your heart be set free of sorrow.

۵۳. کند کاشانه ات آباد به نیک نامی در ایسرایل

53 May she embellish your home,
With a good name among the [people] of Israel.

شلح گوئل، شلح گوئل، زخوت نابی یقوتیئل

Send us redemption, Send us redemption,
In the merit of our prophet, Yeghutiel.

۵۵. آقا حاتان نجیب زاده خدا تاجی به سر داده

55 Master groom, the noble one,
The Lord has crowned you.

۵۶. چو این کلاّ بتو داده شوید پیر وبهم خوشدل

56 Because He has given you this bride,
May you age together and make each other happy.

شلح گوئل، شلح گوئل، زخوت نابی یقوتیئل

Send us redemption, Send us redemption,
In the merit of our prophet, Yeghutiel.

۵۸. به پای هم شوید دلشاد بگیرید کام و هم بنیاد

58 May you make each other joyful,
May the heart's desire be the cornerstone (of your life).

۵۹. که صیون هم شود آباد در او گیریم همه منزل

59 So that Zion also be prosperous,
For us all to have our home.

شلح گوئل، شلح گوئل، زخوت نابی یقوتیئل

Send us redemption, Send us redemption,
In the merit of our prophet, Yeghutiel.

۶۱. همه یاران و غم خواران علم داران و سرداران

61 All friends and companions,
All those who are exalted and leaders.

۶۲. به بزم آیید سرود خوانان برای قوم ایسرایل

62 All singers join in our celebration,
For the sake of the people of Israel.

شلح گوئل، شلح گوئل، زخوت نابی یقوتیئل

Send us redemption, Send us redemption,
In the merit of our prophet, Yeghutiel.

۶۴. در این هفت روز که تو شاهی و هم سلطان و آقایی

64 For these seven days that you are king,
As well as sultan and lord.

۶۵. هر آن خدمت که فرمایی بجا آریم بجان و دل

65 Any command that you give,
We will obey, heart and soul.

شلح گوئل، شلح گوئل، زخوت نابی یقوتیئل

Send us redemption, Send us redemption,
In the merit of our prophet, Yeghutiel.

۶۷. در این هفت روز تو آزادی   به بزم و عیش بپردازی

67 In these seven days you are free,
To spend time in celebration and pleasure.

۶۸. ولی خود را نیاندازی   ز رسم دینِ ایسرایل

68 But may you not disengage yourself,
From the traditions and faith of Israel.

شلح گوئل، شلح شلح گوئل، زخوت نابی یقوتیئل

Send us redemption, Send us redemption,
In the merit of our prophet, Yeghutiel.

۷۰. ز حکم قادر یکتا   که تا یک سال تو باهمتا

70 Following the command of the Almighty,
You need to spend a whole year with your mate.

۷۱. شوید مشغول بر عیش،   تا ببینید خیر در ایسرایل

71 Be engaged in pleasure,
And enjoy the good life [according to the traditions] of Israel.

شلح گوئل، شلح گوئل، زخوت نابی یقوتیئل

Send us redemption, Send us redemption,
In the merit of our prophet, Yeghutiel.

۷۳. بشو خشنود به همزادت   نصیب این خدا دادت

73 Be happy with your soul mate,
With whom the Lord has blessed you.

۷۴. ترا همراه فرستادت   همان سلطان ایسرایل

74 You have been sent a partner,
By the Lord of the [people] Israel.

شلح گوئل، شلح گوئل، زخوت نابی یقوتیئل

Send us redemption, Send us redemption,
In the merit of our prophet, Yeghutiel.

۷۶. علم واری، بلندم کن   اگر زشتم، پسندم کن

76 Like a banner raise me up,
Make me pleasant if I am ugly.

۷۷. اگر تلخم، چو قندم کن   میانِ جمع ایسرایل

77 If I am bitter, make me sweet as sugar,
Among the people of Israel.

شلح گوئل، شلح گوئل، زخوت نابی یقوتیئل

Send us redemption, Send us redemption,
In the merit of our prophet, Yeghutiel.

۷۹. هَشِم باشد به تو یاور   شوند خشنود پدر مادر

79 May the Lord assist you,
May your mother and your father be happy with you.

۸۰. مدام باشی سر و سرور   میانِ جمعِ ایسرایل

80 May you always be the chief and leader,
Among the people of Israel.

شلح گوئل، شلح گوئل، زخوت نابی یقوتیئل

Send us redemption, Send us redemption,
In the merit of our prophet, Yeghutiel.

۸۲. هَشِم باشد آبا تو یار — بگردد نسل تو بسیار

82 May the Lord be friends with you, assist you,
May your offspring multiply.

۸۳. زخوت پینحاسِ العازار — که اوست ماغن به ایسرایل

83 On the merit of Pinhas, the son of Eliezer,
Whose merit guards the [people] of Israel.[37]

شلح گوئل، شلح گوئل، زخوت نابی یقوتیئل

Send us redemption, Send us redemption,
In the merit of our prophet, Yeghutiel.

۸۵. کَلاّ خانم رخش گلزار — پری بطنش همه پُر دار

85 May your bride's face be lively like a flower field,
And may her womb be houseful of fruit.[38]

۸۶. که آرَد پور مثال نار — دوازده پور همه یک دل

86 So that she bears you many sons,
Twelve sons, all of the same heart.[39]

شلح گوئل، شلح گوئل، زخوت نابی یقوتیئل

Send us redemption, Send us redemption,
In the merit of our prophet, Yeghutiel.

۸۸. ببخشاید به تو داور — دوازده پورِ نام آور

88 May the Ruler, the Lord bless you,
With twelve prominent sons.

۸۹. ترا حقّ یار و هم یاور — علم گردی به ایسرایل

89 May the Divine Truth, be your Lord and ally,
May you always be recognized among the [people] of Israel.

شلح گوئل، شلح گوئل، زخوت نابی یقوتیئل

Send us redemption, Send us redemption,
In the merit of our prophet, Yeghutiel.

۹۱. شود عمرت چو بن عمرام — [عمران] شوی دلشاد ز فرزندان

91 May your life be long like [Moses] the son of Amram[Amran],
And you become joyous with children.

۹۲. چو یعقوب نبی پُر دان — بکام دل در ایسرایل

92 May you become so blessed, like Jacob,
And become happy in Israel.

شلح گوئل، شلح گوئل، زخوت نابی یقوتیئل

Send us redemption, Send us redemption,
In the merit of our prophet, Yeghutiel.

37 The Hebrew term "מאג'ן"(maghen/ماغن) means "shield and guardian" in English.
38 The Hebrew term "פרי" (peri/پری) means "fruit" in English.
39 A reference made to the twelve sons of Jacob.

ندا آمد که یا موسی   بگیر در دست تو این عصا ۹۳.

94 A revelation spoke to Moses,
"Take your staff in your hand."

برو در مصر بکن نِس ها   برای قومِ ایسرایل ۹۴.

95 "And go to Egypt to deliver miracles.
For the People of Israel."

شلح گوئل، شلح گوئل، زخوت نابی یقوتیئل

Send us redemption, Send us redemption,
In the merit of our prophet, Yeghutiel.

رسید موسی لبِ دریا   بدید دشمن قفا ناگاه ۹۶.

97 Once Moses reached to the seashore,
Suddenly he saw the enemy behind.

بزد ناله، بگفت الله   از این دریا بده گوئل ۹۷.

98 Crying to the Lord, he asked for redemption,
To be sent so he is saved from the sea.

شلح گوئل، شلح گوئل، زخوت نابی یقوتیئل

Send us redemption, Send us redemption,
In the merit of our prophet, Yeghutiel.

ندا آمد که یا موسی   چه وقتِ ناله است اینجا ۹۹.

100 Revelation came to Moses telling him,
"This is not the time for supplication."

بگیر در دست همان عصا   در این دریا منم گوئل ۱۰۱.

101 "Take your staff in your hand and be ready,
For I am your redeemer through the sea."

شلح گوئل، شلح گوئل، زخوت نابی یقوتیئل

Send us redemption, Send us redemption,
In the merit of our prophet, Yeghutiel.

نبی بشنید بشُد خشنود   عصا بر دست بشد بر رود ۱۰۳.

103 As the Prophet heard this, he became happy,
And entered the sea holding the staff in hand.

به ده جاده که حقّ فرمود   که تا دشمن شود نوفل ۱۰۴.

104 The Lord opened ten paths in the sea,
In order to have their enemies collapse.[40]

شلح گوئل، شلح گوئل، زخوت نابی یقوتیئل

Send us redemption, Send us redemption,
In the merit of our prophet, Yeghutiel.

چه گویم وصفِ بن عمرام   گزینِ خواهر چنان میریام ۱۰۶.

106 How could I portray the son of Amram[Amran],
Without mentioning Miryam, the distinct sister [of his].

40 The Hebrew term "נופל" (nofel/نوفل) means "fallen".

۱۰۷. برون آوردمان زآن یام شیرا گفتند برای "اِل"

107 The Lord, who brought us out of the sea,
Prayers were sung in His honor.[41]

شلح گوئل، شلح گوئل، زخوت نابی یقوتیئل

Send us redemption, Send us redemption,
In the merit of our prophet, Yeghutiel.

۱۰۹. شود آباد بیت همیقداش حخامیم ها کنند داراش

109 May the Holy Temple be rebuilt,
Where the clerics be preaching from.[42]

۱۱۰. سُد توراه بگردد فاش "مُقبض نیدحه" ایسرایل

110 Revealing the hidden secrets of the Torah,
All Israel will be gathered together.[43]

شلح گوئل، شلح گوئل، زخوت نابی یقوتیئل

Send us redemption, Send us redemption,
In the merit of our prophet, Yeghutiel.

۱۱۲. همه آنها که در خوابند شوند بیدار و دریابند

112 May all who have been asleep,
Awaken and realize the truth.

۱۱۳. ز نور حقّ همی تابند که ماییم قومِ ایسرایل

113 On behalf of the glory of the Lord,
We proudly affirm that we are the people of Israel.

شلح گوئل، شلح گوئل، زخوت نابی یقوتیئل

Send us redemption, Send us redemption,
In the merit of our prophet, Yeghutiel.

۱۱۵. ز تو یکتا همی خواهیم دوست و دشمن کُنی از هم

115 We all pray to you, the Divine One,
To differentiate between us and our enemies.

۱۱۶. سوی میقداش رویم با هم کوهن لوی و ایسرایل

116 And lead us all toward the Holy Temple
All together: the Cohens, the Levis, and [other] children of Israel.

شلح گوئل، شلح گوئل، زخوت نابی یقوتیئل

Send us redemption, Send us redemption,
In the merit of our prophet, Yeghutiel.

۱۱۸. همه هستیم به این امید ببینیم روی بن داوید

118 We all share the hope of,
Witnessing the face of the son of David.

41 The Hebrew word "אל" (El/اِل) is a reference to the Lord; the Hebrew term "יאם" (yam/یام) means "the sea".

42 The Hebrew term "דארשׁ"(darash/داراش) means "sermon".

43 This verse refers to Isaiah 56:8, which says: "Thus says the Lord God, who gathers the exiled back to Israel".

۱۱۹. امید ما نَشَد نومید   آید گوئل به ایسرایل

119 May our hope not be dashed,
May redemption come to [people of] Israel.

شلح گوئل، شلح گوئل، زخوت نابی یقوتیئل

Send us redemption, Send us redemption,
In the merit of our prophet, Yeghutiel.

۱۲۱. گئولاه را ظاهر گردان   مکن ما را تو سرگردان

121 Make the redemption apparent,
And do not leave us wandering.

۱۲۲. دشمن ها را تو نیست گردان   رسان ما را به ایسرایل

122 May you annihilate our enemies,
Deliver us to the land of Israel.

شلح گوئل، شلح گوئل، زخوت نابی یقوتیئل

Send us redemption, Send us redemption,
In the merit of our prophet, Yeghutiel.

۱۲۴. فرست بر ما گئولاه را   ببخش بر ما یشوعا را

124 Send us redemption,
And bless us with "salvation".

۱۲۵. ببر بر شهر خود ما را   که تا گیریم در او منزل

125 Lead us to our own town,
Where we can dwell in.

شلح گوئل، شلح گوئل، زخوت نابی یقوتیئل

Send us redemption, Send us redemption,
In the merit of our prophet, Yeghutiel.

۱۲۷. خدای قادرِ سبحان   ماشیح را بما برسان

127 The almighty and pure Lord,
End the redeemer to us.

۱۲۸. از این گالوت مان برهان   زند شوفار زِروبابِل

128 Free us from this Exile,
And have Zerubbabel blow the Shofar.[44]

شلح گوئل، شلح گوئل، زخوت نابی یقوتیئل

Send us redemption, Send us redemption,
In the merit of our prophet, Yeghutiel.

۱۳۰. اگر ما خود گنه کاریم   شفاعت خواه بسی داریم

130 Though we are guilty of sin,
We have many conciliators.

۱۳۱. چو موسی پیرِ حقّ داریم   نمی ترسیم ز هیچ عارل

131 With Moses as our sage,
We have no fear form any infidel.[45]

44 Zerubabel was the leader of the Jews, who were sent back to Jerusalem by Cyrus the Great.
45 The Hebrew term "עארל" ('Arel / عارل) means "not circumcised" in English.

شلح گوئل، شلح گوئل، زخوت نابی یقوتیئل

Send us redemption, Send us redemption,
In the merit of our prophet, Yeghutiel.

۱۳۳. در آن ایام که او آید — در رحمت چو بگشاید

133 At the time of the arrival of our redeemer,
Opening the door of mercy.

۱۳۴. دیگر گالوت نفرماید — کسی بر قوم ایسرایل

134 No Exile leader will have the power,
[To rule over] Jewish people.

شلح گوئل، شلح گوئل، زخوت نابی یقوتیئل

Send us redemption, Send us redemption,
In the merit of our prophet, Yeghutiel.

۱۳۶. ماشیح سوی ما آید — گئولاه تا ابد پاید

136 The redeemer will come to us,
Our redemption will be everlasting.

۱۳۷. شود هادی و بنماید — ره تحقیق به هر "شوئل"

137 As our mentor, he will be guide and direct us,
Towards the Truth, answering all questions.

شلح گوئل، شلح گوئل، زخوت نابی یقوتیئل

Send us redemption, Send us redemption,
In the merit of our prophet, Yeghutiel.

۱۳۹. بیت همیقداش شود آباد — ازین گالوت شویم آزاد

139 The Holy Temple will be rebuilt,
We shall be free from this exile.

۱۴۰. رویم خانه شویم دلشاد — ز نور خاصّ ایسرایل

140 We go to our home land with joy,
With the special glow of [people of] Israel.

شلح گوئل، شلح گوئل، زخوت نابی یقوتیئل

Send us redemption, Send us redemption,
In the merit of our prophet, Yeghutiel.

۱۴۲. همه آییم به دلخواهی — به دو چشمان بینایی

142 We will all come willingly,
Vigilant with our own eyes.

۱۴۳. در هِخال بگشایی — برای قومِ ایسرایل

143 And you open up the arc of the Torah,
To all the people of Israel.

شلح گوئل، شلح گوئل، زخوت نابی یقوتیئل

Send us redemption, Send us redemption,
In the merit of our prophet, Yeghutiel.

۱۴۵. تورای ما بود کامل — شما ای ملت عاقل

145 Our Torah is perfect,
O you, wise people,

۱۴۶. ره ساطان کنید باطل   خوشا بر قوم ایسرایل

146 Nullify the path of Satan,
How good it is for the people of Israel.

شلح گوئل، شلح گوئل، زخوت نابی یقوتیئل

Send us redemption, Send us redemption,
In the merit of our prophet, Yeghutiel.

۱۴۸. آقا "حاتان" مبارک باد   هشم پشت و پناهت باد

148 O bridegroom, congratulations,
May the Lord bless you and stay with you.

۱۴۹. عروست شاد و خرم باد   به نیک نامی در ایسرایل

149 May your bride be happy and cheerful,
With good reputation among [the people] of Israel.

شلح گوئل، شلح گوئل، زخوت نابی یقوتیئل

Send us redemption, Send us redemption,
In the merit of our prophet, Yeghutiel.

Mystic Poetry

סאקינאמה
ساقی نامه
Saqināmeh[46]

1. דוש דר צ'פ'ה צפ'א בודם   בא כה גוים כה דר כ'גִא בודם
2. פרדה דאראן כ'אץ אן דר גאה   הר זמאן מיזדנד בר מן ראה
3. הר זמאני בה פרדהאי דיגר   מן דגר אמדם ז פרדה בה דר
4. גֶר חגִאב מן אז מיאן בר כ'אסת   דר פס פרדה כאר דל שד ראסת
5. גִאן ו דל הר דו המנפ'ס גשתנד   בנדה בגד'אשתנד ו בגד'שתנד
6. דר גֶנאן חאלתי כה מידאני   פרדה אי מאנד פיש עמראני
7. פס אן פרדה דלברי דידם   פרדה בר דאשתם נתרסידם
8. דל גֶו כרד אין דלאו'רי בניאד   גִאן ו דל יאפ'תנד כאם ו מראד
9. תא רך' יאר באזבין דידם   אז כ'וד ו כ'ויש ו יאר ב'ברידם

۱. دوش در صُفّه صفا بودم   با که گویم که درکجا بودم

1 Last night, I was at the palace of purity,
In whom should I confide where I was?

46 Netzer, "Adabiyat-e Yahud-e Iran", pt. 1, pp. 99–106: by 'Emrāni.

۲. پرده داران خاص آن در گاه   هر زمان می زدند بر من راه

2 The prime guards to the divine place,
Blocked me every step of the way.

۳. هر زمانی به پرده ای دیگر   من دگر آمدم ز پرده به در

3 At each obstacle I invented a new trick,
And emerged whole from their obstacle.

۴. چو حجاب من از میان بر خاست   در پس پرده کار دل شد راست

4 Once my veil of the self was removed,
The path before my heart was all clear.

۵. جان و دل هر دو هم نفس گشتند   بنده بگذاشتند و بگذشتند

5 My heart and soul began to breathe as one,
They ascended together, leaving my body behind.

۶. در چنان حالتی که میدانی   پرده ای ماند پیش عمرانی

6 At that pinnacle of awareness,
A veil still remained before ‘Emrāni.

۷. پس آن پرده دلبری دیدم   پرده بر داشتم نترسیدم

7 Behind the veil I spotted a heart-ravishing beloved,
But without fear I removed the veil.

۸. دل چو کرد این دلاوری بنیاد   جان و دل یافتند کام و مراد

8 Once my heart found courage,
My heart and soul fulfilled her wish and desire.

۹. تا رُخ یار نازنین دیدم   از خودِ خویش و یار ببریدم

9 As I beheld the face of the darling Beloved,
I was cut off from my own self and my loved ones.

דר נעת מוסי כלים אללה עליה אלסלאם
درنعت موسی کلیم الله علیه السلام
In Praise of Moses the Conversant, Peace be Upon Him[47]

1. אלא אי ג'רקהי קרקאב ג'פ'לת   גֶראיי אין גֶנין דר גֶאה ג'פ'לת
2. בש'ד ע'מר ו תו כיי דריאבי אכ'ר   גֶה מיגורי מגר דר כ'ואבי אכ̇ר
3. המאנא תרך מ'לך כ'ויש גפ'תי   כה דל בר מרג בנהאדי ו כ''פ'תי
4. בסא דרדי כה דרמאנש נב'רדנד   כה אכ'ר אנדר אן עלת במרדנד
5. כסי רא אגהי בכ'שנד אז כ'ויש   כה ברדארד תגֶאב כ'ויש אז פיש
6. נגרדד אהרמן אכ'ר סליימאן   נדאנד הר סליימאן נ'טק מרג'אן
7. תו גר כ'ואהי כה אין מעני בדאני   אזין ט''למת תן כ'וד וא רהאני
8. חגֶאב כ'ויש רא אז פיש ברדאר   כה תא גרדי ז ראה כ'וד כ'ברדאר
9. יכיש'דפישש־ייכ'יכאיכ'רדמנד   מרא אנדר חקיקת דה יכי פנד
10. גֻואבש דאד שיך' נאם ברדאר   בב'ר אז כ'ויש בא חק בשוו יאר
11. תו תא באשי גרפ'תאר עלאיק   כגֶא גרדי בה כ'ייל דוסת לאיק

47 ‘Emrāni, *Fatḥnāmeh*, m.s. BZI 964: f. 6b.

12. חגֿאב ראה תו דאם גֿהאן אסת נפנדארי כה אינגֿא אשיאן אסת
13. גֿהאן באכסו'פ'אדארי נכרד אסת פ'לך בא כס היץ' יארי נכרד אסת

۱. آلا ای غرقهٔ قَرقابِ غفلت چرائی این چنین درچاهِ غفلت

1 Thou penetrated in the trench of ignorance,
Why are you dumped in this ditch?

۲. بِشد عمُرو تو کی دریابی آخر چه میگوئی مگر در خوابی آخر

2 Your life is passed and when would you find at last,
What do you have to say, are you asleep?

۳. همانا تَرکِ مُلکِ خویش گفتی که دل بر مرگ بنهادی و خفتی

3 In fact you have departed from your own "self",
By your acceptance of the sleep of ignorance.

۴. بسا دردی که درمانش نبردند که آخر اندر آن علت بمردند

4 Finding no cure for their pain,
Many died because of their pain.

۵. کسی را آگهی بخشند از خویش که بردارد حجاب خویش از پیش

5 The people who get to know their own "self",
Are those who remove the barrier facing them.

۶. نگردد اهرمن آخر سلیمان نداند هر سلیمان نطق مرغان

6 Satan at no time turn into Solomon,
Not every Solomon knows the language of the birds.

۷. تو گر خواهی که این معنی بدانی ازین ظلمت تن خود وارهانی

7 If you want to know the meaning [of the Truth],
And rescue yourself from dark ignorance.

۸. حجاب خویش را از پیش بردار که تا گردی ز راه خود خبردار

8 Remove the barrier of your own "self",
To know the secret of your pathway.

۹. یکی شد پیش شیخی کای خردمند مرا اندر حقیقت ده یکی پند

9 Approaching the wise sage, one asked,
For an advice to find the Truth.

۱۰. جوابش داد شیخِ نام بردار بُبر از خویش با حق بشو یار

10 The response of the eminent sage was,
Depart from your own "self" to accompany the Truth.

۱۱. تو تا باشی گرفتار علایق کجا گردی به خیلِ دوست لایق

11 As long as you are entangled with corporal attachments,
How can you be capable of joining the crowd of the "Friend"?

۱۲. حجاب راه تو دام جهان است نپنداری که اینجا آشیان است

12 The barrier on your way is your corporal trap,
Do not ever think this place is your nest.

۱۳. جهان با کس وفاداری نکردست فلک با کس هیچ یاری نکردست

13 The world has never been loyal to anyone,
The Universe, with not one, has never kept its friendship.

צופ'יאן כ'יר כ'ואה
صوفیانِ خیر خواه
The Well-Wishing *Ṣufis*[48]

1. כ'ייר כ'ואה ו פישו'א סאלך ו הם מקתדא   האדי גם כרדה ראה צופ'יאנד צופ'יאן
2. כ'וש אדא ו פ'ר עטא מקבל שאה ו גדא   עפ'ו'כ'ואה הר כ'טא צופ'יאנד צופ'יאן
3. מסתגֿאםדרקצדגֿאןאזעשקדידארנהאן   דאדהכפ'האאזענאןצופ'יאנדצופ'יאן

١. خیرخواه و پیشوا سالک وهم مقتدا   هادیگمکردهراه،صوفیانندصوفیان
1 Well-wishers and mentors, who pave and lead the road of the mystics,
Directing those who are lost are the *Ṣufis*, the *Ṣufis*.
٢. خوش ادا و پرعطا مقبل شاه وگدا   عفوخواه هر خطاصوفیانندصوفیان
2 Poised and benevolent, accepted by both the noble and the poor,
forgiveness Seeking for every transgression are the *Ṣufis*, the *Ṣufis*.
٣. مست جام درقصد جان ازعشق دیدار نهان   داده کف ها ازعنان صوفیانند صوفیان
3 Drunk from the goblet, in desire of facing the inner soul, for love of seeing the secret,
Losing self-possession, are the *Ṣufis*, the *Ṣufis*.

מנאגֿאת
مناجات
Prayer[49]

1. איי קאדר קדרת נמא   איי צאנע ערץ' ו סמא
2. הר דם כ'ני רחמי בה מא   איי קאדר קדרת נמא
3. יכתא ו בי המתא תוי   דל כ'וש כ'ן דלהא תוי
4. רוזי דה אשיא תוי   איי קאדר קדרת נמא
5. הפ'ת אסמאן נילגון   בי גֶוב ו בי סנג ו סתון
6. אנדר סר מא הסת נגון   איי קאדר קדרת נמא
7. הפ'ת טאק ו כייו'אן ו פ'לך   גֶבדין הזאראן הם מלך
8. הר יך בה נאמי יך בה יך   איי קאדר קדרת נמא

١. ای قادرِ قدرت نما   ای صانع اَرض و سما
1 O Lord, displaying might,
Creator of heaven and earth,
٢. هردم کنی رحمی بما   ای قادرِ قدرت نما
2 Have mercy on us, day and night,
O Lord displaying might.

48 Simanṭov Melamed, *Ḥayat al-Ruḥ.* ms. 57608o: fol. 84:b. 39.
49 Netzer, *Montakhab*, p. 377: by Shahab Yazdi.

۳. یکتا و بی‌همتا توئی   دل خوش کنِ دل ها توئی

3 You are one, you are peerless,
You who cheers our downcast hearts.

۴. روزی ده اشیاء توئی   ای قادر قدرت نما

4 Providing us with our daily needs,
O Lord displaying might.

۵. هفت آسمان نیلگون   بی چوب و بی‌سنگ و ستون

5 The seven azure domes of heaven,
Without wood, without stone, and without columns,

۶. اندر سرِ ما هست نگون   ای قادر قدرت نما

6 Hover inverted overhead,
O Lord displaying might.

۷. هفت طاق و کیوان و فلک   چندین هزاران هم ملک

7 Seven vaults, celestial bows,
With angels in their thousands filled,

۸. هر یک به نامی یک به یک   ای قادر قدرت نما

8 Each with a name in rows displayed by,
O Lord displaying might.

שאהזאדה ו צופ'י
شاهزاده و صوفی
The Prince and the *Ṣufi*[50]

באב השת'ם דר ביאן אנכה אדמי רא מעני מיבאיד ו נה צורת כה דל מיר'באיד

باب هشتم: در بیان آنکه آدمی‌را معنی می باید و نه صورت که دل می‌رباید

Chapter Eight: Describing the Necessity of Inner Depth for an Individual Rather than an Attractive External Appearance

1. דלא תא כיי בה צורת בגרו'י תו   גֶה באשד גר בה מעני בנגרי תו
2. כה בי מעני ר'ך' צורת נכו ניסת   בג'ז ויי אדמי רא אברו ניסת
3. בה שהזאדה תו'אצ'ע כרד צופ'י   דלש דר מהר ויי כ'ו כרד צופ'י
4. בגפ'תש כאיי תו רא זיבנדה דוולת   מרא ברדאשתי אז כ'אך ד'לת
5. בה רוי מן דר אחסאן גשאדי   מקאם סרו'ראנם גַאי דאדי
6. זגרדון בגד'ראנדי אפ'סרם רא   ז כ'אנאן בר פ'זודי ר'תבתם רא
7. גֶנין דידם טריק אלתפ'אתת   כה שאהי בא דו שכ'ץ זשת הייאת
8. בגפ'תא שאהזאדה כאיי סכ'ן גו   גֶה סאן בודסת תמת'אלש בה מן גו

۱. دلا تا کی به صورت بگروی تو   چه باشد گر به معنی بنگری تو

1 O heart, how long have you been beguiled by looks,
How would it be for you to look at the deep meaning?

50 Netzer, *Montakhab*, p. 323; by Elisha‘ ben Shemuel (Raqeb). This chapter describes the meeting of the Prince, and the Ṣufito explains the features of the two hideous individuals he had seen before.

که بی معنی رُخ صورت نکونیست   بجز وی آدمی را آبرو نیست

2 With no depth, appearances are not pleasant, .۲
Without depth, man has no integrity.

به شهزاده تواضع کرد صوفی   دلش در مهر وی خو کرد صوفی

3 To the prince, the *Ṣufi* extended courtesy, .۳
His heart was filled with affection.

بگفتش کای ترا زیبنده دولت   مرا برداشتی از خاک ذلت

4 Telling him,You worthy of command, .۴
Have released me from disgrace.

به روی من در احسان گشادی   مقام سرورانم جای دادی

5 The doors of kindness you opened to me, .۵
Placed me at the level of eminent grace.

ز گردون بگذراندی افسرم را   ز خانان بر فزودی رُتبتم را

6 Ascending my crown above the universe, .۶
You elevated my rank above the nobles.

چنین دیدم طریق التفاتت   که شاهی با دو شخص زشت هیئت

7 That is how I perceived your kindness, .۷
That you are a ruler faced with two ugly appearances.

بگفتا شاهزاده کای سخن گو   چه سان بودست تمثالش به من گو

8 The Prince asked the sage to describe, .۸
How were his features, tell me that.

Didactic Poetry

מ׳כ׳ממס אז יוסף' בן אסחאק י׳הודי
مُخَمَّس از یوسف بن اسحق یهودی
A Five Hemistich Poem from Yousef b. Esḥāq b. Yahūdī[51]

1. **ז ח'כאמי בה ד'ניא גֻ׳נד ט''לם ו זור מיסאזי   בראי מאל ד'ניא עאלמי דר שור מיסאזי**
2. **דרון סינה אז עדאו'ת גֻ׳נד פרדאזי   גֻ׳ה גֻ׳אהי כנדהאי דר דל כה כ׳לקי אנדר אנדאזי**
3. **נמיתרסי אז אן רוזי כה כ'וד רא דר מיאן ביני**

۱. زحکامی به‌دنیا چندظلم‌وزورمی‌سازی   برای‌مال‌دنیا عالمی‌در شور می‌سازی
۲. درون سینه از عداوت چند پردازی   چه چاهی کنده ای در دل که خلقی اندر اندازی
۳. نمی ترسی از آن روزی که خود را در میان بینی؟

51 Netzer, "Adabiyat-e Yahud-e Iran", pt. 1, p. 75: by Yusef b. Esḥāq b. Yahūdī.

1 With your authority, how can you be so tyrannical and cruel?
For the pleasures of the world, how much grief can you make?
2 How much enmity can you feel in your heart?
What hole have you dug in your heart to dump a whole crowd in?
3 Are you not afraid you will one day see yourself drowned in that hole?

ואג̇באסת ו ארכאן סיזדהגאנה

באב סו'ם דר שנאכ'ת בי ג̇סמי חצ'רת עזת

واجبات وارکان سیزده گانه

باب سوم در شناخت بی جسمی حضرت عزت

The Thirteen Principles of Faith

Chapter Three

Recognition of the Spirituality of His Holiness[52]

1. ו'אג̇באסת ג̇מלה אהל אימאן רא   הר כה או הסת פיירוו תוורא
2. כה ביארד בה ין סכ'ן אימאן   הר כה או הסת בנדה יזדאן
3. כה נדארד כ''דאי בי המתא   ג̇סד ו ג̇סם ו גֶשם ו דסת ו פא
4. ברי אז נ'טק ו צורת ו גוש אסת   בי קד ו קאמת ו בר ו דוש אסת
5. או מ'בראסת אז המה צורת   בשנוו אין גֶנד בית אז חכמת
6. עקל דר ג̇סתג̇וי או חייראן   פ'כר ו אנדישה מאנדה סרגרדאן
7. ג̇'מלה צאלחאן ו בא ראיאן   בא המה כאמלאן ו דאנאיאן
8. מאנדה דר כארגאה או חייראן   כס נכרדה רהי בה אין אייו'אן
9. פ'לך ו כווכב ו ברוג̇ ו ספהר   מלך ו ג̇ן ו אנס ו מאה ו מהר
10. המה תסביח ו ש'כר או גוינד   הר כג̇א אנד דוסת מי ג̇וינד
11. או המה ג̇א ו היץ ג̇אי נה   ד'את או רא גֶה ו גֶראי נה

۱. واجب است جمله اهل ایمان را   هر که او هست پیرو تورا

1 It is necessary for all the believers,
Whoever follows the Torah.

۲. که بیارد به این سخن ایمان   هر که او هست بندۀ یزدان

2 That he believes in this speech,
Whoever is obedient to the Lord;

۳. که ندارد خدای بی همتا   جسد و جسم و چشم و دست و پا

3 That the incomparable Creator has no
Corpse and body, eyes, hands, and feet.

۴. بری از نطق و صورت و گوش است   بی قد و قامت و بر و دوش است

4 With no mouth, face and ear,
With no stature, height, chest and shoulder.

۵. او مبراست از همه صورت   بشنو این چند بیت از حکمت

5 He is far from every kind of face,
Listen to these few verses of wisdom:

52 Netzer, *Montakhab*, p. 240: by ‘Emrāni.

۶. عقل در جستجوی او حیران   فکر و اندیشه مانده سرگردان

6 Reason is bewildering in the quest to find him,
Thoughts and contemplations have gone astray.

۷. جمله صالحان و با رایان   با همه کاملا ن و دانایان

7 All the righteous and intellectuals,
Along with those perfect and wise,

۸. مانده در کارگاه او حیران   کس نکرده رهی به ا ین ایوان

8 Are amazed by his miracles,
No one could find a way to this door.

۹. فلک و کوکب و بروج و سپهر   مَلَک و جِن و اِنس و ماه و مهر

9 The cosmos and stars, constellations and the skies,
From angels and fairies to humans, the moon and the sun,

۱۰. همه تسبیح شکر او گویند   هر کجا اند دوست می جویند

10 They all praise Him with gratitude,
Wherever they are, in search of the beloved.

۱۱. او همه جا و هیچ جائی نه   ذات او را چه و چرائی نه

11 His presence is everywhere and nowhere,
His true essence needs no question and inquiry.

Panegyric Poetry

דר מדח ס'לטאן אל מ'עט'ם אבו סעיד כ'אן
در مدح سلطان المعظم ابوسعید خان
In Eulogy of the Honorable Sultan Abu Saeed Khan[53]

1. ס'לטאן גִהאן שה מ'עט'ם   כ'ורשיד מ'עט'ם ו מכרם
2. שהזאדה אבו סעיד סלטאן   דארנדה תאגִ ו תכ'ת דווראן
3. אזאדה בהאד'ר גִהאנגיר   קתתאל עדו בה ראי ותדביר
4. בגרפ'ת גִהאן בצ'רב שמשיר   מאו'אי עדו בכרד סר זיר
5. אנדר בר או גֶה בזם גֶה רזם   בא נצרת או גֶה רזם גֶה בזם
6. דר רזם גֶו שיר נר כרושד   בא בבר והז'בר בר כ'רושד
7. צד צפ' שכנד בה צ'רב כופאל   דר גאה ילי גֶו רסתם זאל
8. דר בזם הזאר חאתם טיי   דר ראה סכ'א ניאמדש פיי
9. פייו'סתה בה עדל ו דאד כושד   בר תכ'ת בסי נביד נושד
10. סווגנד שהאן בו'ד בה תאגִש   בר פ'יל כשד המה כ'ראגִש

53 Netzer, *Montakhab*, pp. 113–114: *Ardashīrnameh* by Shāhīn.

۱. سلطان جهان شه معظم   خورشید معظم و مُکَرَم

1 Sultan of the world, exalted king,
The magnificent and honorable sun,

۲. شه زاده ابو سعید سلطان   دارندۀ تاج و تخت دوران

2 Son of the king, Abu Saeed, the sultan,
Owner of the crown and throne of our age.

۳. آزاده بهادر جهانگیر   قتّال عدو به رای و تدبیر

3 The noble hero, world conqueror,
Who brings down the head of his foes with wisdom and will.

۴. بگرفت جهان به ضرب شمشیر   مأوای عدو بکرد سر زیر

4 He conquered the world with the blow of his sword,
Making his enemy's homeland subservient to his own.

۵. اندر بر او چه بزم چه رزم   با نصرت او چه رزم چه بزم

5 At his throne, whether in banquet or combat,
At his victory, whether in combat or banquet.

۶. در رزم چو شیر نر خروشد   با ببر و هُژبر بر خروشد

6 In combat, he roars like a fiery lion,
When facing tigers and lions.

۷. صد صف شکند به ضرب کوپال   در گاه یلی چو رستم زال

7 Breaking hundreds with his mace,
At the time of heroism like Rostam, son of Zal.

۸. در بزم هزار حاتم طی   در راه سخا نیامدش پی

8 In banquets he is thousand times that of *Ḥatam Ṭaiee* [the benevolent],
In generosity, no one can best him.

۹. پیوسته به عدل و داد کوشد   بر تخت بسی نبید نوشد

9 Constantly engaged in justice and fairness,
Ample wine he drinks, while on his throne.

۱۰. سوگند شهان بود به تاجش   بر فیل کشد همه خراجش

10 To his crown is the pledge of kings,
Carried by elephants are ransoms paid to him.

דר נעת מוסי כלים אללה עליה אלסלאם
درنعت موسی کلیم الله علیه السلام
In Praise of The "Conversant" Moses, Peace be Upon Him[54]

1. שה באז גִהאן גֻראג' דידה   מוסי כלים בר ג'זידה
2. סימרג' פ'ראז ק'להי טור   סרמסת כ'טאב ו שיר ג'פ'ור
3. דאנבדהי ראז לן תראני   נור דל ו דפ'תר מעאני
4. שהבאז סכ'א، רסול דאו'ר   בדר כרם אפ'תאב כ'או'ר

54 Netzer, *Montakhab*, p. 110: *Ardashīrnameh* by Shāhīn.

5. גנגֿו'ר שריעת אלאהי   פ'כ'ר נסב ו תבאר שאהי
6. מנשור סראדוקאת קדרת   סרדאר אמין וכ'אץ חצ'רת
7. סר דפ'תר דאנש ו תריקת   מקבול מכ'אזן ו חקיקת
8. דאו'ר גֿו בה צבח שאם או כרד   אז גֿאר חרוף' נאם או כרד
9. מימש זמכארם כרם בוד   ו'או'ש ז ו'קאר נור מעבוד
10. סינש ז סכ'או'ת גֿהאנבאן   יאיש ז יקין בו'ד בה סבחאן

۱. شه باز جهان چراغِ دیده   موسی کلیم برگزیده

1 The royal falcon of the world, the light of the eye,
Moses, the chosen Conversant,

۲. سیمرغ فراز قُلهٔ طور   سرمست خطا ب و شیر غفور

2 The eagle of Mount Sinai,
Intoxicated by the address, the merciful lion.

۳. دانندهٔ راز لَن ترانی   نور دل و دفتر معانی

3 Aware of the secret of the unseen,[55]
Light of the heart and the book of meanings.

۴. شهباز سخا رسول داور   بَدر کرم آفتاب خاور

4 The falcon of generosity, the prophet mediator,
The full moon of generosity, the sunshine of the East.

۵. گنجورِ شریعتِ الهی   فخرِ نسب و تبارِ شاهی

5 Treasurer of divine law,
Pride of the lineage of the royal dynasty.

۶. منشورِ سرادِقات قدرت   سردارِ امین و خاصّ حضرت

6 The charter of the threshold of power,
The trusted and exclusive commander of the Exalted.

۷. سر دفتر دانش و طریقت   مقبول مخازن حقیقت

7 The exordium of the book of knowledge and faith,
Accepted by the sources of truth.

۸. داور چو به صبح شام او کرد   از چار حروف نام او کرد

8 By daybreak, the Lord lightened his night,
Formed his name Moses by these four letters:

۹. میمش ز مکارم کرم بود   واوش ز وقار نور معبود

9 The "mim" [m] is for the grandeur of his nobility,
And the "vaav" [v] is for the dignity of the light of the Beloved.

۱۰. سینش ز سخاوت جهانبان   یایش ز یقین بود به سبحان

10 The "sin" [s] is for the generosity of the world guardian,
And the "ya" [y] for belief in the Gloried.

55 A reference to Exodus 33:18-23: Then Moses said, "Now show me your glory." And the Lord said, "I will cause all my goodness to pass in front of you, and I will proclaim my name, the Lord, in your presence. I will have mercy on whom I will have mercy, and I will have compassion on whom I will have compassion. But," he said, "you cannot see my face, for no one may see me and live."

דר נעת הארון עליה אלסלאם
در نعت هارون علیه السلام
In Praise of Haroun, Peace be Upon Him[56]

1. דאנאי ג̇האן חלים דאו'ר   הארון כה בו'ד אפ'תאב כ'או'ר
2. אגאה ג̇האן אמאם מעצום   נאדידה ג̣ו דידה כרד מעלום
3. שה באז ו ג̣ראג' נסל יעקוב   אז רה נפ'ס נגשתה מג'לוב
4. מקבול אחד כ'לאצה דין   עאלי נסבי בה ראי ו תמכין
5. פירוז פיי כ''ג̇סתה דידאר   פ'תתאח ו כליד גנג̇ אסראר
6. מיימון קדם ו סלים בא דאד   ג̇ייחון כרם ו חלים בניאד
7. צאדר ז תבאר אל עמראן   נור אזלי ג̣ראג' צבחאן
8. אסודה נהאד כוב כרדאר   ו'אקף שדהי כ'טאב ו אסראר
9. דסתור צדור חט'רת ראז   מה טלעת פ'ר דל ו סר אפ'ראז
10. סרדאר מקאם ברג̇ מיעאד   ביג̣ארה נו'אז דל פ'ר אז דאד
11. דאנא בג̇האן דגר ג̣ו הארון   נאמד ז מכאן לטף בירון

۱. دانای جهان حلیم داور   هارون که بوَد آفتاب خاور

1 The sage of universe, the tolerant judge,
Aaron, who was the sun from the East.

۲. آگاه جهان امام معصوم   نادیده چو دیده کرد معلوم

2 Cognizant of the world, the immaculate leader,
Revealed the unseen just as the seen.

۳. شه باز و چراغ نسل یعقوب   از ره نفس نگشته مغلوب

3 The royal falcon and the light of Jacob's successors,
Never defeated for the sake of ego.

۴. مقبول احد خلاصهٔ دین   عالی نسبی به رای و تمکین

4 Accepted by the Lord, a profile of the faith,
Of noble origin, for wisdom and dignity.

۵. پیروز پی خجسته دیدار   فتاح و کلید گنج اسرار

5 Of triumphant origin and auspicious sight,
Opener and the key to the treasure of secrets.

۶. میمون قدم و سلیم با داد   جیحون کرم و حلیم بنیاد

6 Blessed of power and sound with justice,
Flowing with generosity like the Oxus river and of duteous foundation.

۷. صادر ز تبار آل عمران   نو ر ازلی چراغ سبحان

7 Inheritor of Amram[n]'s family,
Gloriously shining with the Lord's eternal light.

۸. آسوده نهادِ خوب کردار   واقف شدهٔ خطاب و اسرار

8 Free character of righteous deeds,
Knower of both seen and unseen knowledge.

56 Netzer, *Montakhab*, p. 112: *Ardashīrnameh* by Shāhīn.

۹. دستور صدور حضرت راز   مه طلعت پُر دل و سرافراز

9 The minister who issues decrees with divine justice,
The moon faced, exalted of the sun-like heart.

۱۰. سردار مقام برج میعاد   بیچاره نواز دل پر از داد

10 Eminent general of the promised pinnacle,
Caresser of the desperate with a heart full of justice.

۱۱. دانا بجهان دگر چو هارون   نامد زمکان لطف بیرون

11 No sage in the world compares to Aaron,
Or has yet emerged from that place of divine favor.

Satirical Poetry

הרגז נבנדי דל בה זן
هرگز نبندی دل به زن
Never Attach Your Heart to a Woman[57]

1. איי דל ביא בשנוו זמן   איי נור גֶשם גִאן מן
כ'ואהי נמירי בי כפ'ן   הרגז נבנדי דל בה זן
2. גר רוי או באשד קמר   באשד לבש המגֶון שכר
בשנוו זמן גִאן פדר   הרגז נבנדי דל בה זן
3. גר דכ'תר קייצר בו'ד   גיסוש אגר ענבר בו'ד
חסנש זמה בהתר בו'ד   הרגז נבנדי דל בה זן
4. גר גֶשם מסתש נסתרין   דוור לבאנש אנגבין
גר כ'אל דארד בר גִבין   הרגז נבנדי דל בה זן
5. גר קד או באשד בלנד   אברוי או באשד כמנד
הרגֶנד באשד דלפסנד   הרגז נבנדי דל בה זן
6. הרגז בה סוי זן מרוו   רנבאל זן הרגז מרוו
פנד אמינא רא שנוו   הרגז נבנדי דל בה זן

۱. ای دل بیا بشنو زمن   ای نور چشم جان من
خواهی نمیری بی کفن   هرگز نبندی دل به زن

1 Oh my heart, come and listen to me,
You the light of my soul,
If you do not wish to be buried without a shroud,
Never attach your heart to a woman.

57 Netzer, "Adabiyat-e Yahud-e Iran", part 1: by Aminā (Benjamin ben Mishael).
The term مستزاد (*Mostazad*) refers to a poem in which the second hemestich in every two lines is repeated.

۲. گرروی او باشد قمر باشد لبش همچون شکر
بشنو زمن جان پدر هرگز نبندی دل به زن

2 If her face resembles the moon,
Her sweet lips are like sugar,
Take my words, my beloved son,
Never attach your heart to a woman.

۳. گر دختر قیصر بود گیسوش اگر عنبر بود
حسنش زمه بهتر بود هرگز نبندی دل به زن

3 If she is Caesar's daughter,
If her ringlets are like ambergris,
And her beauty outshines the moon,
Never attach your heart to a woman.

۴. گرچشم مستش نسترین دور لبانش انگبین
گرخال دارد برجبین هرگز نبندی دل به زن

4 If her rose-like eyes are intoxicating,
And her sweet lips are covered with honey,
If she has a beauty mark on her forehead,
Never attach your heart to a woman.

۵. گر قد او باشد بلند ابروی او باشد کمند
هرچند باشد دلپسند هرگز نبندی دل به زن

5 If she is tall in height,
If she has curved eyebrows like bowstrings,
No matter how pleasant she is,
Never attach your heart to a woman.

۶. هرگز بسوی زن مرو دنبال زن هرگزمرو
پند امینا را شنو هرگز نبندی دل به زن

6 Never approach a woman,
Never pursue a woman,
Listen to Amina's advice,
Never attach your heart to a woman.

Different Vocabularies and Ethnicities

פארסי מיאנה
پارسی میانه
Judeo-Persian and Middle Persian

Judeo-Persian has been recognized by linguistic scholars of the Persian language as a conduit between Middle Persian and New Persian owing to numerous grammatical peculiarities revealed in Judeo-Persian writings. As Gilbert Lazard puts it, although Judeo-Persian writings do not differ from Persian writings in general, they often contain linguistic information not found elsewhere. In addition to dialectical and grammatical points, such particularities include a large number of Middle Persian morphemes and vocabulary. *Fatḥnāmeh*, a 15th-century New Persian text, still reflects some such characteristics. The following are examples of terms rooted in Middle Persian used by ʻEmrāni.

ו'אז'גאן פארסי מיאנה
واژگان پارسی میانه
Middle Persian Vocabulary

.1 **אייו'אר / ایوار**/ evening or late afternoon:[58]

כה תא רוזי ז פ'רמאן גְהאנדאר   רסידנד דר יריחו ו'קת **אייו'אר**
که تا روزی ز فرمان جهان دار   رسیدند در یریحو وقت ایوار

At such time, with the Lord's providence,
They arrived at Jericho by early evening.

.2 **בייו'ר/ بیور**/ten thousand:[59]

בדיד אן כ'יימה ו כ'רגאה לשכר   ספאה בי כראן אפ'זון ז **בייו'ר**
بدید آن خیمه و خرگاه لشکر   سپاه بی کران افزون ز **بیور**

He saw the tent and military pavilion,
An enormous army, exceeding ten thousand.

ו'אז'גאן תרכי
واژگان ترکی
Turkic Cultural Terms and Concepts

During the Mongol rule in Iran of the 13th century, in the Il-khanid era, we find Mongol terms and culture penetrating to Iranian language, literature, and arts.

ג'ד'אהי תרכי
ترکی غذاهای
Turkish Food Items and Dishes

.1 **בקרא**/بُقرا/ a dish after Boqra Khan, an Ilkhanid ruler؛ **כומאגְ**/کوماج/ Kind of bread:

אבא מאהיגֶה ו **בקרא** ו **כומאגְ**   דל ו רוח ו רואן רא כרד תאראגְ
آبا ماهیچه و **بُقرا** و **کوماج**   دل و روح و روان را کرد تاراج

With shanks, *boqra* and *Kumaj*,
Were the heart and soul and mind invaded.[60]

58 ʻEmrāni, *Fatḥnāmeh*, ms. BZI, 964 fol. 94a: 8.
59 ʻEmrāni, *Fatḥnāmeh*, ms. BZI, 964 fol. 94a: 8.
60 ʻEmrāni, *Fatḥnāmeh*, ms. BZI, 964 fol. 70a: 12. Dekhoda: Boqra is the Turkish name for a Mongol dish. Kumaj, also of Turkish origin, refers to a kind of bread baked over a fire in a metal pan.

ו'אז'גאן זבאן תרכי
واژگان زبان ترکی
Turkic Vocabulary

1. **גֿאו'ושאן**/**چاووشان**/ the army commanders:

רו'אן גשתנד **גֿאו'ושאן** בה תעגיל   בה קאמת הר יכי אפ'זון ז יך מיל
روان گشتند **چا ووشان** به تعجیل   به قامت هر یکی افزون ز یک میل

The commanders started out in a hurry,
Each one's height was beyond measure.[61]

זבאן ו מפ'אהים ערבי ו אסלאמי
زبان و مفاهیم عربی و اسلامی
Arabic Language and Islamic Concepts

Judeo-Persian texts include Arabic words reflecting the social life, knowledge and usage of such vocabulary by Iranian Jews.

ג'ד'אה ו מו'אד כ'ראכי ערבי
غذاها و مواد خوراکی عربی
Arabic Food Items and Dishes

1. **קליה**/ **قليه**/ a casserole kind of a dish; **מזעפ'ר**/**مزعفر**/ (flavored with zafaran):

אבש בא נכ'וד אב ו **קליה** בר סר   שהנשאהי המה נעמת **מזעפ'ר**
آبش با نخودآب و **قليه** بر سر   شهنشاهی همه نعمت **مزعفر**

The soup with peas and chopped vegetable,
All royal meals seasoned with Saffron.[62]

נאמאהי ערבי
Arabic Names
نام های عربی

The Arabic versions of some biblical names, including the name of the Lord, are used in many Judeo-Persian works, to replace or parallel the Hebrew or Persian versions:

1. **אלאה**/ **الله**/ the Lord:

ז צנע ו קדרת ו תקדיר **אללה**   נבודנד אגה אן קומאן גמראה
ز صُنع و قدرت و تقدیر **الله**   نبودند آگه آن قومان گمراه

Of the Lord's creation, power, and divine providence,
Those lost people were not aware.[63]

61 'Emrāni, *Fatḥnāmeh*, ms.BZI, 964 fol. 18a: 12.
62 'Emrāni, *Fatḥnāmeh*, ms. BZI, 964 fol. 70a: 11.
63 'Emrāni, *Fatḥnāmeh*, ms. BZI, 964 fol. 36b: 17.

2. בני יעקוביאן / بنی یعقوبیان/ Israelites or Bnai Jacob:

בני יעקוביאן רא אגהי דאד   שדנד אן קוום אז אן כ'נדאן ו דלשאד

بنی یعقوبیان را آگهی داد   شدند آن قوم از آن خندان و دلشاد

He made the Israelites aware,
For which that nation was happy and pleased.[64]

3. מוסי כלים[אללה] موسی کلیم [لله]/ Moses or the Conversant with the Lord:

בחק רפ'עת ערש עט'ימת   בחק תרבת **מוסי כלימת**

بحق رفعت عرش عظیمت   بحق تربت **موسی کلیمت**

To your glorious divine rule,
To the dust of your conversant Moses.[65]

4. מוסי ו הארון / موسی و هارون/ Moses and Aaron:

נגהדאריד תרתיבש בקאנון   בה אייני כה **מוסי** כרד ו **הארון**

نگهدارید ترتیبش به قانون   به آیینی که **موسی** کرد و **هارون**

Observe His law as ordered,
In the manner set up by Moses and Aaron.[66]

מפ'אהים אסלאמי
Islamic Concepts
مفاهیم اسلامی

1. תסביח ו תהליל/ تسبیح و تهلیل/ praised be the Lord:

בה **תסביח** ו **תהליל** גְהאנבאן   בדנד דר ו'גְד אן גְמע אמאמאן

به **تسبیح** و **تهلیل** جهانبان   بُدند در وجد آن جمع امامان

In praise of the Lord of the universe,
Those people were in ecstasy.[67]

2. רב אלעאלמין/ ربّ العالمین/ the Lord of the Universe:

יקין אן לטף' **רב אלעאלמין** אסת   בדאניד איי סראפ'ראזן גְנין אסת

یقین آن لطفِ **ربّ العالمین** است   بدانید ای سرافرازان چنین است

Be assured that it is the grace of the Lord,
Know ye, O nobles, that it is thus.[68]

3. סייד מ'רסל / צדר אמאמת/ the honorable prophet/Head of prophecy/ **سیّدِ مرسل/صدرِ امامت**:

בדין **סייד מ'רסל** תמאמת   דלאלת כרדשאן **צדר אמאמת**

به دینِ **سیّد مرسل**، تمامت   دلالت کردشان **صدرِ امامت**

To the faith of the honorable prophet,
The head of prophecy directed them all.[69]

64 ʻEmrāni, *Fatḥnāmeh*, ms. BZI, 964 fol. 30a: 2.
65 ʻEmrāni, *Fatḥnāmeh*, ms. BZI, 964 fol. 89a: 6. ʻEmrāni, *Fatḥnāmeh*, ms. BZI, 964 fol. 36b: 17.
66 ʻEmrāni, Fatḥnāmeh, ms. BZI, 964 fol.11a: 31.
67 ʻEmrāni, Fatḥnāmeh, ms. BZI, 964 fol. 39a: 7.
68 ʻEmrāni, Fatḥnāmeh, ms. BZI, 964 fol.19b:26.
69 ʻEmrāni, Fatḥnāmeh, ms. BZI, 964 fol.70a:2.

זבאן עברי ו מפ'אהים יהודי

زبان عبری و مفاهیم یهودی

Hebrew Language and Judaic Concepts

One of the three major points that make Judeo-Persian writings distinct from other types of writing in Persian literature—both in prose and verse—is the use of Hebrew vocabulary:

1. **צדאקאה/ صِداقاه/** :charity/donation:

דו דסתם דר **צדאקאה** כ'ו גר כן   מרא אנדר כרם צאחב הנר כן

دو دستم در **صِداقاه** خوی گر کن   مرا اندر کرم صاحب هنر کن

Make my hands accustomed to giving alms,
Make me proficient in charity.[70]

2. **ארון/آرون/** :Holy Ark, where the Torah scrolls are kept:

בגפ'ת אין ו בכוהנאן בפ'רמוד   כה בר דאריד **ארון** רא ז גַא זוד

بگفت این و بکوهنان بفرمود   که بر دارید **آرون** را ز جا زود

Saying this, he then ordered the Cohens,
To quickly pick up the Holy Ark.[71]

3. **צנדוק שהאדאת/صندوق شهادات/** : the Holy Covenant carried in a case:

כ'רדמנדאן ו דאנאיאן תוראת   נגהדאראן **צנדוק שהאדאת**

خردمندان و دانایانِ تورات   نگهدارانِ **صندوق شهادات**

The elders and those well versed in the Torah,
Those preservers of the Holy Ark.[72]

4. **אבו'ות ו עראו'ות/ آبوت و عراووت/** :fathers, heavenly:

כ'דאו'נדא בחק **אבות**   בחק כרסי ערש **עראו'ות**

خداوندا به حق **آووت**   به حق کرسی عرش **عراووت**

O Lord, I pray thee for my fathers' sake,
For The sake of the seat in divine court[73].

5. **תאגַ תוראה/ تاج تورا/** :the crown of the Torah, a literary translation of a Jewish Midrash

זדי **תאגַ תוראה** בר סר מן   מרא נגד'אשתי בר כאם דשמן

زدی **تاج تورا** بر سر من   مرا نگذاشتی بر کام دشمن

You have crowned me with the crown of the Torah,
By not deserting me, or leaving me to my enemies.[74]

6. **זכ'ות /زخوت/** :merit, divine, virtue:

נכ'סתין אז **זכ'ות** שאפ'ע מא   כלים אללה גַראג' דין ו דניא

نخستین از **زخوت** شافع ما   کلیم الله چراغ دین و دنیا

First by the divine virtue of our intercessor,
Moses, the light of earth and heaven.[75]

70 'Emrānī, Fatḥnāmeh, ms. BZI, 964 fol.BZ3b:6
71 'Emrānī, Fatḥnāmeh, ms. BZI, 964 fol. 23b:7.
72 'Emrānī, *Fatḥnāmeh*, ms. BZI, 964 fol. 40b:6.
73 'Emrānī, *Fatḥnāmeh*, ms. BZI, 964 fol. 4a:2.
74 'Emrānī, *Fatḥnāmeh*, ms. BZI, 964 fol. 11a:8.
75 'Emrānī, *Fatḥnāmeh*, ms. BZI, 964 fol. 32a: 10.

.7 **סכאנאה/ سکاناه/** danger, harm:

الف: בה חכם אן אגאזת דאד מעבוד כה אישאן רא **סכאנאה** אנדר אן בוד
به حکم آن اجازت داد معبود که ایشان را **سکاناه** اندر آن بود

a With that order, the Lord gave permission,
Since there was harm for them, in that[76].

ب: הר אן אמרי כזאן כ'יזד **סכאנאה** נבאיד כרד פ'תו'א דאד תורה
هر آن امری کزان خیزد **سکاناه** نباید کرد، فتوی داد توراه

b The action which would cause danger,
The Torah has ordered not to be committed.[77]

Literary Terms

.1 **قُلزُم / ק'לז'ם** / a sea or a wide river:

الف: פ'ראת ו דגלה דר פאיש פ'תאדה סר אנדר **ק'לז'ם** ו גייחון נהאדה
فرات و دجله در پایش فتاده سر اندر **قُلزُم** و جیحون نهاده

a Euphrates and Tigris are at his feet,
They both have joined the Oxus river.[78]

ب: דר אן מדת כה גבבאר גהאנבאן ב קדרת כרד **ק'לז'ם** גון ביאבאן
در آن مدت که جَبّار جهانبان بقدرت کرد **قُلزُم** چون بیابان

b At the time when the Lord of the universe,
Dried out the wide sea into a desert.

.2 born at the conjunction of two happy stars, fortunate/title of kings:
צאחבקראן /صاحبقران/

אגר גה סרו'ר ו **צאחבקראן** בוד נבי ו שהריאר ו כאמראן בוד
اگرچه سرور و **صاحبقران** بود نبی و شهریار و کامران بود

Even though he was a leader and royalty,
He was a prophet, a ruler, and a fortunate one.[79]

76 'Emrānī, *Fatḥnāmeh*, ms. BZI, 964 fol. 32a: 4.
77 'Emrānī, *Fatḥnāmeh*, ms. BZI, 964 fol. 32a: 5.
78 'Emrānī, *Fatḥnāmeh*, ms. BZI, 964 fol.17a:5; 19a:2; fol.17b: 14.
79 'Emrānī, *Fatḥnāmeh*, ms. BZI, 964 fol.17b: 14.

3. ק'רה באז/ قُرّه باز/ rider of a black horse:

בזירש **ק'רה באזי** באד רפ'תאר   כה גַ'רך' או רא נדידי ו'קת פייכאר
به زیرش قُرّه **بازی** باد رفتار   که چرخ او را ندیدی وقت پیکار

He was a swift, wind-like horse rider,
The universe had never seen one like him in battle.[80]

מפ'אהים חמאסי ו קהרמאנאן א'סתורהאי
Epic Concepts and Legendary Heroes
مفاهیم حماسی و قهرمانان اُسطوره ای

1. קמר ו מהר /قمر و مهر/ the sun and the moon taking military orders:

קמר דר דלו' בוד ו **מהר** דר ת'ור   ז אמר חק באיסתאדנד דר דוור
כ'טאב אומד נבי רא פיש גַבבאר   בר או'רדם מראדת רא דגר באר
قمر در دلو بود و **مهر** در ثور   ز امر حق بایستادند در دور
خطاب اومد نبی را پیش جبّار   بر آوردم مرادت را دگر بار

The moon was in Aquarius and the sun was in Taurus,
Upon the Lord's order, they stopped their heavenly circumambulation.
The Prophet was addressed by the Almighty, saying:
"I have responded your wish once again".[81]

2. רויין תן/ رویین تن/ arrow-proof body of the epic hero Rostam:

המה **רויין תן** ו פולאד פייכר   המה אהן דל ו גרד ו הנרור
همه **رویین تن** و پولاد پیکر   همه آهن دل و گرد و هنرور

All invulnerable and solid in body,
All iron in heart, brave, and virtuous.[82]

3. אספ'נדיאר/ תהמתן/ביז'ן / اسفندیار/ تهمتن/ بیژن epic characters Esfandiyar, Tahamtan and Bijan:

בה גרדי הר יכי **אספ'נדיארי**   **תהמתן** צפ'דרי **ביז'ן** תבארי
به گُردی هر یکی **اسفندیاری**   **تهمتن** صفدری **بیژن** تباری

In heroism, they each are like Esfandiyar,
Each brave and valiant, descendants of Bijan.[83]

4. כוה קאף'/ کوه قاف/ legendary mountain in epic and other literary works:

בה נסבת מלך מן גַ'ון כוה **קאף'** אסת   כה רא דר **קאף'** אמכאן מצאף' אסת
به نسبت ملک من چون کوه **قاف** است   که را در **قاف** امکان مصاف است

In comparison, my land is as high as peak of Qaff,
A mountain which no one has yet encountered.

80 'Emrāni , *Fatḥnāmeh*, ms. BZI, 964 fol. 85a:2.
81 'Emrāni, *Fatḥnāmeh*, ms. BZI, 964 fol. 89a: 18; 90b:1.
82 'Emrāni, *Fatḥnāmeh*, ms. BZI, 964 fol. 100b: 13.
83 'Emrāni, *Fatḥnāmeh*, ms. BZI, 964 fol. 97a: 9.

5. **רכ'ש** /**رَخش**/: legendary horse of the hero Rostam

בה רוז כין זין בר **רכ'ש** בנדם   ניארד גִסת רסתם אז כמנדם

به روز کین زین بر **رَخش** بندم   نیارد جَست رستم از کمندم

On the day of battle, once I place my saddle on Rakhsh,
Even Rostam cannot stay free of the loop of my lasso.[84]

6. دارا /**דארא**/: name of a just king of the Acheamenid dynasty

כ'בר דאריד **דאראי** דאו'ר   כה בוד או פאדשאה הפ'ת כשו'ר

خبر دارید **دارای** داور   که بود او پادشاه هفت کشور

Do you know of the ruler Dara,
Who was the king of seven countries?[85]

7. **אסכנדר**/ **اسکندر**/ Alexander:

ז **אסכנדר** נינדישיד דר גִנג   הם אכ'ר פיש או בספרד אוורנג

ز**اسکندر** نیندیشید در جنگ   هم آخر پیش او بسپرد اورنگ

He was not fearful of Alexander,
To the point that he lost his throne to him.[86]

8. **בהמן** ו **זאל** /**بهمن** و **زال**/ Bahman and Zal:

שנידיד איי ילאן אסראר **בהמן**   כה בהר באב שד בא **זאל** דשמן

شنیدید ای یلان اسرار **بهمن**   که بهر باب شد با **زال** دشمن

You warriors, have you heard the secrets of Bahman,
Who, in every way possible, made an enemy of Zal?[87]

9. **זאבל**/**זאל**/ **בהמן** /**زابل** ، **زال** ، **بهمن**/names of cities and heroes:

גִה אמד סוי **זאבל** בר סר **זאל**   בה **בהמן** כ'נדה מיזד **זאל** בא יאל

چه آمد سوی **زابل** بر سر **زال**   به **بهمن** خنده میزد **زال** با یال

What happened to Zal on the way to Zabol?
Zal, with his white mane who was smiling at Bahman.[88]

10. **אפ'סון** ו **ניירנג** /**افسون** و **نیرنگ**/deceit and treachery:

הם אכ'ר בהמן אז **אפ'סון** ו **ניירנג**   גרפ'תש דר קפ'ס כרדש גהי גִנג

هم آخر بهمن از **افسون** و **نیرنگ**   گرفتش در قفس کردش گهی جنگ

But Bahman, by deceit and trickery,
Arrested [Rostam–e Zal] and put him in chains. [89]

84 ‘Emrāni, *Fatḥnāmeh*, ms. BZI, 964 fol.27a:2.

85 ‘Emrāni, *Fatḥnāmeh*, ms. BZI, 964 fol.60a: 15. Dara, the Persian emperor, known for his justice.

86 ‘Emrāni, *Fatḥnāmeh*, ms. BZI, 964 fol.60a: 16.

87 ‘Emrāni, *Fatḥnāmeh*, ms. BZI, 964 fol.60a: 18.

88 ‘Emrāni, *Fatḥnāmeh*, ms. BZI, 964 fol. 100b: 19.

89 ‘Emrāni, *Fatḥnāmeh*, ms. BZI, 964 fol.60a: 19.

מפ'אהים זרתשתי
Zoroastrian Concepts
مفاهیم زرتشتی

Judeo-Persian poets, like some other Iranian poets, often interpret Zoroastrian dualism as a non-monotheist belief, thus symbolically refer to non-believers as Zoroastrians.

1. פ'רר/فرّ/ :divine providence

الف: **זפ'רר** ו צדמת אן שיר גִבבאר   תמאמת כאפ'ראן רסתנד זאן כאר
ز **فرّ** و صدمت آن شیر جبّار   تمامت کافران رستند زان کار

a From the divine providence and strength of that lion-like hero,
All infidels were saved by running away from the battle.[90]

ب: כ'וש אמד שאה רא דידאר דאו'וד   כמאל ו דאנש ו גפ'תאר דאו'וד
גִו'אני דיד בא **פ'רר** ו הדאית   דליר ו כארדאן ו בא דראית
خوش آمد شاه را دیدار داوود   کمال و دانش و گفتار داوود
جوانی دید با **فرّ** و هدایت   دلیر و کاردان و با درایت

b The king was pleased with the sight of David,
His excellence, knowledge and eloquence,
He saw a youth with divine glory and leadership,
Brave, competent and intelligent.[91]

2. זנד ו פאזנד/ زند و پازند/ Abridged and translation of *Avesta* at two different intervals called Zand and Pazand:

בכפ'ר ו כאפ'רי דל כרדה כ'רסנד   מקייד גשתה בהר **זנד** ו **פאזנד**
بِه کفر و کافری دل کرده خرسند   مقید گشته بهر **زند** و **پازند**

They are content with disbelief,
They have committed themselves to their books, Zand and Pazand.[92]

3. גבר/گبر/ :Zoroastrian, also used for idol worshiper

الف: חלאלסת כ'ון **גבראן** רא תמאמת   שמא רא ניסת אז אן אכנון מלאלת
حلالست خون **گبران** را تمامت   شما را نیست از آن اکنون ملامت

a) Blood of the pagans is totally permissible,
You are not to be blamed for that now.[93]

ب: בגו תא דר יריחו אנדר אינד   בה **גבראן** דסתברדי ו'א נמאינד
بگو تا در یریحو اندر آیند   به **گبران** دست بردی وا نمایند

b) Tell them to raid the city of Jericho,
To plunder the non-believers.[94]

90 ʻEmrāni, *Fatḥnāmeh*, ms. BZI, 964 fol. 383a: 12; 280a: 5-6.
91 ʻEmrāni, *Fatḥnāmeh*, BZI, 964 fol. 280a:6
92 ʻEmrāni, *Fatḥnāmeh*, BZI, 964 fol. 65a: 13. *Zand* and *Pazand*, the translation and re-translation of Avesta.
93 ʻEmrāni, *Fatḥnāmeh*, ms. BZI, 964 fol. 29b: 7.
94 ʻEmrāni, *Fatḥnāmeh*, ms. BZI, 964 fol. 39b:5.

ג: בכרדנד מאל **גבראן** רא בג'ארת   בברדנד דר פיש צאחב אמארת
بکردند مال **گبران** را بغارت   ببردند در پیش صاحب امارت

c) They plundered the belongings of the non-believers,
Taking them all to their commander.[95]

4. אהרמן/ اهرمن/ :evil, Satan
נגרדד **אהרמן** אכ'ר סליימאן   נדאנד הר סליימאן נטק מרג'אן
نگردد **اهرمن** آخر سلیمان   نداند هر سلیمان نطق مرغان

The Devil will never turn into Solomon,
Not every Solomon knows the language of the birds.[96]

Rhetorical Arts

אסתעארה האי חמאסי
استعاره های حماسی
Epic Metaphors

1. תיג' ג'ם /تیغ غم/:the sword of sorrow
כה תא אז **תיג' ג'ם** אסודה גרדי   מבאדא נאגהאן פ'רסודה גרדי
که تا از **تیغ غم** آسوده گردی   مبادا ناگهان فرسوده گردی

In order to be free from the sword of sorrow,
You should never get burned out.[97]

2. תיג' כ'ורשיד ו תב מריך'/ تیغ خورشید و تب مریخ / :the sword of the sun and the temper of Mars
כשידה **תיג' כ'ורשיד** דר שב   ז תאב תיג'שאן **מריך'** דר **תב**
کشیده **تیغ خورشید** در شب   ز تاب تیغشان در **تب مریخ**

With the sword of the sun pulled out at night,
Mars in fever from the glow of their sword.[98]

3. זלף' סנאן /زُلف سِنان/ :the curl of a spear
יכי שמשיר ב'רראן אב מידאד   יכי **זלף' סנאן** רא תאב מידאד
یکی شمشیر بُرّان آب می داد   یکی **زُلف سِنان** را تاب میداد

Someone was sharpening his trenchant sword,
While another one was twisting his spear's tip.[99]

95 'Emrāni, *Fatḥnāmeh*, ms. BZI, 964 fol. 42a: 1.
96 'Emrāni, *Fatḥnāmeh*, ms. BZI, 964 fol. 6b: 6.
97 'Emrāni, *Fatḥnāmeh*, ms. BZI, 964 fol. 42b: 1
98 'Emrāni, *Fatḥnāmeh*, ms. BZI, 964 fol. 55a: 4.
99 'Emrāni, *Fatḥnāmeh*, BZI, 964 fol. 68b: 1.

4. שמשיר כין/شمشیر کین/ :the Sword of hatred

כנון **שמשיר כין** רא תיז סאזיד   בה כין אין סתמכאראן בתאזיד
کنون **شمشیر کین** را تیز سازید   به کین این ستمکاران بتازید

Now sharpen the sword of hatred,
And strike the tyrants in revenge.[100]

אסתעארה האי תג'זזלי
استعاره‌های تغزّلی
Lyric Metaphors

1. רכ'ת זמרד /رختِ زمرد/ :emerald clothing

גֿמן **רכ'ת זמרד** כרדה דר בר   ריאחין תאגֿ זר כרדה בר סר
چمن **رخت زمرد** کرده در بر   ریاحین تاج زر کرده بر سر

The grass has worn the emerald clothes,
The aromatic plants have crowned themselves with golden crowns.[101]

2. זלף' בנפ'שה/زلفِ بنفشه/ :the ringlets of violets

גהי **זלף' בנפ'שה** תאב דאדי   גהי חסן ריאחין אב דאדי
گهی **زلف بنفشه** تاب دادی   گهی حسن ریاحین آب دادی

Sometimes the wind curls up the ringlets of violets,
Sometimes it leaves drops of dew on the aromatic plants.[102]

3. גֿעד גֿמן /جعدِ چمن/ :curls of grass

גהי ארג'ואן סנבל שאנה כרדי   גהי **גֿעד גֿמן** רא שאנה כרדי
گهی ارغوان سنبل شانه کردی   گهی **جعد چمن** را شانه کردی

Sometimes the Judas tree combed the hair of the hyacinths,
Sometimes it combed the curls of grass.[103]

4. שמע גֿאן/ شمعِ جان/ :candle of the soul

בה אימאן **שמע גֿאן** רא בר פ'רוזיד   בתאן רא גֿמלה דר אתש בסוזיד
به ایمان **شمع جان** را برفروزید   بتان را جمله در آتش بسوزید

Light the candle of life with faith and belief,
Burn all idols in the fire.[104]

5. ערוס מהר ו אינה מה/ :the bride of the sun and the mirror of the moon
عروسِ مهر و آینهٔ مَه/

ערוס מהר גֿון רו רא עיאן כרד   פ'לך **אינה מה** רא נהאן כרד
عروس مهر چون رو را عیان کرد   فلک **آینهٔ مه** را نهان کرد

Upon the bride of the sun showing her face,
The heavens hid the mirror of the moon.[105]

100 ʻEmrāni, *Fatḥnāmeh*, BZI, 964 fol. 29b: 4.
101 ʻEmrāni, *Fatḥnāmeh*, BZI, 964 fol. 29b: 5.
102 ʻEmrāni, *Fatḥnāmeh*, ms. BZI, 964 fol. 21b: 22.
103 ʻEmrāni, *Fatḥnāmeh*, ms. BZI, 964 fol. 21b: 24.
104 ʻEmrāni, *Fatḥnāmeh*, ms. BZI, 964 fol. 25a: 18.
105 ʻEmrāni, *Fatḥnāmeh*, ms. ORD, 13704 fol. 147:2.

גנאס תאם
جناس تام
Homophony[106]

:pearl **مروارید/گوهر /גוהר/**paralleled with /pure essence/**اصل و ریشه /گوهر/ גוהר** .1

כסי **גוהר** ברון ארד אזין אב   כה באשד **גוהרש** גון **גוהר** נאב

کسی **گوهر** برون آرد ازین آب   که باشد **گوهرش** چون **گوهرناب**

That person who can bring the pure pearl out of the water,
Their nature is as pure as the pearl itself. [107]

:opportunity /**غنیمت** /**ג'נימת**/ paralleled with/ booty /**غنیمت**/ **ג'נימת** .2

ג'נימת רא **ג'נימת** מי שמרדנד   אז אנהא הר יכי בכ'שי בברדנד

غنیمت را **غنیمت** می شمردند   از آنها هر یکی بخشی ببردند

They seized opportunity from the booty,
Everyone got a share of it.[108]

:hard (adj.) /**سخت**/ **סכ'ת**/ paralleled with / very (adv.) **سخت/ סכ'ת** .3

בה שאהאן גפ'ת הוראם נגון בכ'ת   כה בר מא כאר אסאן שד **סכ'ת סכ'ת**

به شاهان گفت هورام نگون بخت   که بر ما کار آسان شد **سخت سخت**

The unfortunate Huram told the kings
That for us, the easy simple job has become very difficult.[109]

גנאס כ'טטי
جناس خطی
Scriptural Homophony[110]

:fast /**جُست**/ **גִ'סת**/ paralleled with fast (adj)/ **چُست/גֻ'סת**/ .1

נה הר כוו שנאו'ר באשד ו **גֻסת**   תו'אנד גוהר אנדר בחר הא **גִ'סת**

نه هر کو شناور باشد و **چُست**   تواند گوهر اندر بحرها **جُست**

Not everyone who can swim and is fast,
Is capable of finding pearls in the sea.[111]

: arrow/**تیر**/ **תיר**/ paralleled with / old/**پیر**/ **פיר** .2

זן ו פ'רזנד ו טפ'ל ו כודך ו **פיר**   כשידה אז ניזה ו שמשיר ו אז **תיר**

زن و فرزند و طفل و کودک و **پیر**   کشیده از نیزه و شمشیر و از **تیر**

Woman, child, infant, and elder,
All suffered from the spear, sword, and arrow.[112]

106 When two words are written and pronounced the same way with different meanings.
107 ʻEmrāni, *Fatḥnāmeh*, ms. BZI, 964 fol. 10b:18.
108 ʻEmrāni, *Fatḥnāmeh*, ms. BZI, 964 fols. 90b:9, 93a:8; ms. KZ127: 10.
109 ʻEmrāni, *Fatḥnāmeh*, ms. BZI, 964 fol. 98:18
110 When only the dots are different, giving a different meaning
111 ʻEmrāni, *Fatḥnāmeh*, ms. BZI, 964 fol. 10B: 16.
112 ʻEmrāni, *Fatḥnāmeh*, ms. BZI 964 fol. 29b:9.

3. גֿאה /جاه/ גֿאה/ چاه / paralleled with /position /جاه/ **גאה** /well:

גרפ'תאר טמע גרדיד נאגאה ז **גֿאה** או נאגהאן אפ'תאד דר **גֿאה**

گرفتار طمع گردید ناگاه ز **جاه** او ناگهان افتاد در **چاه**

He suddenly became entangled in greed,
He suddenly fell from a lofty position into a well.[113]

4. גֿאן / جان / paralleled with / soul / **כ'אן / خان [خانه]** / home:

אמיד אז **גֿאן** ו **כ'אן** ו מאן ברידנד רה בירון שדן גֿאיי נדידנד

امید از **جان** و **خان** و مان بریدند ره بیرون شدن جایی ندیدند

They gave up the hope of life, a home and possessions,
Not finding any way out.[114]

גֿנאס נאקץ

جناس ناقص

Incomplete Homophony[115]

1. סאיה / سایه / shadow / paralleled with / **דאיה/ دایه** / wet nurse:

פ'כנדה פ'אכ'תה בר סר **סאיה** ג רפ'תש סרו' אנדר בר גֿו **דאיה**

فکنده فاخته بر سرو **سایه** گرفتش سرو اندر بر چو **دایه**

The ringdove cast its shadow upon the cypress,
The cypress embraced it like a wet nurse.[116]

2. כ'אן / خان [خانه] / home / paralleled with / **מאן / مان** / possession:

אמיד אז גֿאן ו **כ'אן** ו **מאן** ברידנד רה בירון שדן גֿאיי נדידנד

امید ازجان و **خان** و**مان** بریدند ره بیرون شدن جائی ندیدند

They gave up the hope of having life, a home and possessions,
Not finding any way out.[117]

3. בכ'ת / بخت / fortune / paralleled with/ **סכ'ת / سخت** / difficult:

בה שאהאן גפ'ת הוראם נגון **בכ'ת** כה בר מא כאר אסאן שד סכ'ת **סכ'ת**

به شاهان گفت هورام نگون **بخت** که بر ما کار آسان شد سخت، **سخت**

To his rulers, the unfortunate Huram said,
What we though simple, has become extremely tough work.[118]

4. זאל / زال / an epic hero / paralleled with / **יאל / یال** / mane:

גֿה אמד סוי זאבל בר סר **זאל** בה בהמן כ'נדה מיזד **זאל** בא **יאל**

چه آمد سوی زابل بر سر **زال** به بهمن خنده میزد **زال** با **یال**

113 ‘Emrāni, *Fatḥnāmeh*, ms. BZI, 964 fol. 51a:13.

114 ‘Emrāni, *Fatḥnāmeh*, ms. BZI, 964 fol. 58b:14.

115 When there is only one letter different between the two words.

116 ‘Emrāni, *Fatḥnāmeh*, ms. BZI, 964 fol. B: 21b:21.

117 ‘Emrāni, *Fatḥnāmeh*, ms. BZI, 964 fol. 58b:14.

118 ‘Emrāni, *Fatḥnāmeh*, ms. BZI, 964 fol. 58b:14.

Rhythmic Embellished Prose

חיאת אל רוח נו'שתה סימן טוב מלמד

حيات الروح نوشته سيمانطوب ملمد

Simanṭov Melamed[119]

במשרפ'אן כ'הן ומערופ'אן ס'כ'ן וטאלאבאן כרם ומחרמאן חרם רא ס'כ'ן מכ'פ'י ניסת ונמאנד כה איגַאד כאינאת מכ'צוץ ו'גוד אדמי בר פא שדה ואדם אן כס רא גוינד כה פ'רק ניך ובד יעני ד'ניאי פ'אני ועקבאי גַאו'דאני רא דריאפ'תה באשד ובג'ייר אין חאל אן שכ'ץ רא בהאים כו'אננד ובלכ'ם כמתר.....

[ואין פ'קיר חקיר] אז סִר צדק גַאן כ'ואהש נמוד כה כתאבי בנא כ'נם כה חאגַת סלים אל-נפ'סאן זמאנה בה אגַאבת רסד[תא] אז גַאם אצלי ו'ז שרבת אזלי מחרום נמאננד ובאז פ'כר נפ'סאני מאנע שד יעני[גפ'ת] גֶון תו כסי קאדר בה אין קדרת ניסתי בה אין גֶנין דרה'י בי פאיאן קדם נהי וגר קדם נהי, סר דר באזי ואין גֶנין אמרי רא שכ'ץ מדרך ומערופ'י ס'כ'ן סנג באיד ועאקלאן גפ'תהאנד לקמה קאלב דהן ומערפ'ת נסבת בס'כ'ן מ'ו'אפ'ק ט'אבטה בו'ד ותרא נפ'עי נרסד מגר אפ'סוס משפ'קאן וטען. אחמקאן

به مشرفانِ كهن و معروفانِ سخن و طالبانِ كرم و محرمانِ حرم را سخن مخفى نيست و نماند كه ايجاد كاينات مخصوص وجود آدمى برپا شده و آدم آن كس را گويند كه فرقِ نيک و بد، يعنى دنياى فانى و عقباى جاودانى را دريافته باشد و به غيرِ اين حال، آن شخص را بهايِم خوانند و بلكُم كمتر. . . .

و اين فقير حقير] از سر صدق جان خواهش نمود كه كتابى بنا كنم كه حاجتِ سليم النفسانِ] زمانه به اجابت رسد [تا] از جام اصلى وَز شربت اَزَلى محروم نمانند و باز فكَر نفسانى مانع شد؛ يعنى [گفت] چون تو كسى، قادر به اين قدرت نيستى به اين چنين درّهٔ بى پايان قدم نهى و گر قدم نهى، سر دَر بازى و اين چنين امرى را شخصِ مُدرِک و معروفى سخن سنج بايد و عاقلان گفته اند لقمه قالبِ دهن و معرفت نسبتَ به سخن، موافق ضابطه بُوَد، . و ترا نفعى نرسد، مگر افسوسِ مشفقان و طعنِ احمقان.

The universe has been created especially for the existence of human beings. This concept was never concealed from the nobles of antiquity, nor will it be

119 Simanṭov Melamed, *Ḥayat al-Ruḥ*, Ben Ben Zvi Institute, Jerusalem, 5760 8 o, Introduction: fols. 1:a–2a.

from the scholars of letters, seekers of His eminence and those privileged of His sanctity.

The attributes of a human being are bestowed upon those who are capable of differentiating between good and evil, as well as the transitory and eternal world. Otherwise humans are considered equal or even less than beasts. . . .

Thus my soul whole heartedly pleaded for the edition of a book to fulfill the needs of the virtuous as well as the deprived of my time. This effort would enable them to have a taste of the eternal drink from the main cup of Divine Truth.

Once more, my worldly consciousness attempted to divert my thoughts and convince me that a person of my abilities is incapable to step into such an infinite domain. Should I make such an attempt, I will be unable to execute its compilation. Such a mission should be addressed only by an intelligent and prudent individual. As it is said by the sages, it is only appropriate to take a bite to fit one's mouth and to utter a word to fit one's mouth. Otherwise, one is only left with the pity of sympathetic friends and the scorn of fools.

Bibliography

Asiri, Fażl Mahmud. 1950. "Rubaiyat-i Sarmad," in *Visva Baharati 11*. Santiniketan: Visva-Baharati.

Bacher, Wilhelm. 1907. *Zwei Judisch-Perscische Dichter, Schahin und Imrani*. Budapest: Alkalav & Sohn.

Bakhtiari Mahmudi, Behrooz, and Farhang Farid. 2011. "Bārgāh-e Khashāyārshā: Introduction," in *Iran Nameh* 26(3–4): 14–116.

Berquist, Jon L. 1995. *Judaism in Persia's Shadow*. Minneapolis: Fortress Press.

Book of Ezra. 1994. *The New Oxford Annotated Bible with the Apocrypha*. New York: Oxford University Press.

Browne, E.G. 1998. *Literary History of Persia* (four volumes) 2. London: T. Fisher Unwin Ltd.

De Lagarde, Paule. 1884. *Persiche Studien* (Abhandlungen der Koniglichen Gresellschaft der Wissenchaften zu Gottingen) XXXI.

Fānī, Muhsin, 1262. *Dabistan al Mazahib*. Trans. 1846. Bombay.

Farhang-e Mo'in. 1992. Tehran: Amir Kabir Publishers.

Fischel, Walter J. 1971. "Judeo-Persian Literature," in *Encyclopedia Judaica*, vol. 10, 13th ed. Jerusalem: Ketter Publishing House Ltd.

———. 1949. "Israel in Iran (The Genesis of Judeo-Persian Literature)," in *The Jews: Their History, Culture, and Religion*, edited by Louis Finkelstein, vol. 2, 824. Philadelphia: The Jewish Publication Society of America.

———. 1948–49. "Jews and Judaism at the Court of the Moghul Emperors in India," in *Proceedings of the American Academy for Jewish Research*. New York: Ktav Publishing House, Inc.

Gupta, M.G. 1991. *Sarmad, the Saint: Life and Works*. Agra: MG. Publishers.

Horn, Siegfried H. 1999. "The Divided Monarchy: The Kingdoms of Judah and Israel," in *Ancient Israel*, edited by Hershel Shanks, 192–193. Washington, DC: Biblical Archaeology.

Iran Chamber Society. 2014. "Mortza NeyDavoud, Music of Iran," www.iranchamber.com/music/mneydavoud/morteza_neydavoud.php. (Accessed May 1, 2014).

Jewish Virtual Library: Iben Kamuna, Sa'ed Iban Mansur, www.jewishvirtuallibrary.org/jsource/judaica/ejud_0002_0009_0_09416.html. (Accessed May 4, 2014).

Lazard, Gilbert. 1996. "The Dialectology of Judeo-Persian," in *Pādyāvand*, edited by Amnon Netzer, vol. 1. Costa Mesa: Mazda Publishers.

———. 1971. "Judeo-Persian," in *Encyclopedia Judaica*, vol. 10, 13th ed. Jerusalem: Ketter Publishing House Ltd.

Levy, Habib. 1999. *Comprehensive History of the Jews of Iran*. Abridged by Hooshang Ebrami. Translated by George W. Maschke. Costa Mesa: Mazda Publishers.

Loghatnameh-ye-Dehkhoda. 1987. Tehran: Tehran University Press.

Moreen, Vera Bach. 1987. *Iranian Jewry's Hour of Peril and Heroism. A Study of Bābāī Ibn Loṭf's Chronicle (1617–1662)*. New York/Jerusalem: The American Academy for Jewish Research.

______. 2000. *In Queen Ester's Garden*. New Haven/London: Yale University Press.

Netzer, Amnon. 2003. "Jewish Poet Amina of Kashan and His Sacred Poems," in *Irano-Judaica*, edited by Shaul Shaked and Amnon Netzer, vol. 5. Jerusalem: Ben-Zvi Institute.

———. Babai b. Loṭf, www.iranicaonline.org/articles/babai-ben-lotf. (Accessed April 28, 2014)

———. 2002. "An Early Judeo-Persian Fragment from Zefreh," in *Jerusalem Studies in Arabic and Islam*, no. 27. The Hebrew University of Jerusalem.

———. 1999a. "Adabiyat-e Yahud-e Iran", part 2. [Persian Literature], in *Pādyāvand*, edited by Amnon Netzer, vol. 3. Costa Mesa: Mazada Publishers.

———. 1996a. "Adabiyat-e Yahud-e Iran", part 1. [Persian Literature], in *Pādyāvand*, edited by Amnon Netzer, vol. 1. Costa Mesa: Mazada Publishers.

———. 1996b. "Tarikh-e Yahud-e Iran", part 1. [History of Iranian Jews], in *Pādyāvand*, edited by Amnon Netzer, vol. 1. Costa Mesa: Mazda Publishers.

———. 1995. *Duties of Judah by Rabbi Yehudah Ben el'Azar*. Edited, translated and introduced by Amnon Netzer. Jerusalem: Ben Zvi Institute.

———. 1994. "Rashid al-Din and His Jewish Background," in *Irano-Judaica* vol. 3, edited by Shaul Shaked and Amnon Netzer. Jerusalem: Ben Zvi Institute.

———. 1985. *Manuscripts of the Jews of Persia in the Ben-Zvi Institute*. Jerusalem: Ben Zvi Institute.

———. 1974. "A Judeo-Persian Footnote: Shahin and 'Emrani," in *Israel Oriental Studies*, edited by M.J. Kister. Tel-Aviv: Tel Aviv University.

———. 1973. *Montakhab-e Ashār-e Fārsi āz Āsār-e Yahūdīāyān-e Irān* [Selected Persian Poetry, Heritage of the Jews of Iran]. Edited by Amnon Netzer. Tehran: Farhang-e Iran Zamin.

Neusner, Jacob. 2009. "Judeo-Persian communities xii. Persian Contribution to Judaism," in *Encyclopaedia Iranica*, edited by Ehsan Yarshater, vol. 15/2, www.iranicaonline.org/articles/judeo-persians-xii-persian-contribution-to-judaism. Accessed January 27, 2014.

Oxford Annotated Bible, New Revised Standard Version. Oxford: Oxford University Press, 1994.

Pirnazar, Jaleh, 2000. "Iranian Jews, National Identity, and Journalism: 1915–1979," in *The History of Contemporary Iranian Jews*, vol. 4, edited by Homa Sarshar. Beverly Hills: Center for Iranian Jewish Oral History.

Pirnazar, Nahid. 2016. "Sarmad of Kashan: Jewish Saint, Persian Poet," in *Iran Namg* 1(3).

———. 2011. "Habib Levy," in *Jewish Communities of Iran*, edited by Houman M. Sarshar. New York: Columbia University Press.

———. 2004. "The Place of the Fifteenth Century Judeo-Persian Religious Epic 'Emrāni's *Fatḥnāmeh* in Iranian Literary traditions," Doctoral Dissertation. University of California, Los Angeles.
Pourjavady, R., and S. Schmidtke. 2006. *A Jewish Philosopher of Baghdad. 'Izz al-Dawla Ibn Kammuna (d. 683/1284) and His Writings*. Leiden and Boston: E.J. Brill, www.academia.edu/405319/A Jewish_Philosopher of_Baghdad._Izz_al-Dawla_Ibn_Kammuna_d._683_1284_and_His_Writings. (Accessed May 11, 2014) http://plato.stanford.edu/entries/ibn-kammuna/. (Accessed April 25, 2014)
Purvis, James D. 1999. "Exile and Return: From the Babylonian Destruction to the Reconstruction of the Jewish State," in *Ancient Israel*, edited by Hershel Shanks. Washington, DC: Biblical Archaeology.
Rypka, Jan. 1968. "An Outline of Judeo-Persian Literature," in *History of Iranian Literature*, edited by Jan Rypka. Dordrecht: D. Reidel Publishing Company.
Sarhar, Houman. 1997. "Moshfegh Hamedani," in *The History of Contemporary Iranian Jews*, edited by Houman Sarshar. Beverly Hills: Center for Iranian Jewish Oral History.
Secunda, Shai, 2014. *The Iranian Talmud: Reading the Bavli in the Sasanian Context*. Philadelphia: University of Pennsylvania Press.
Secunda, Shai, and Steven Fine. 2012. *Shoshannat Yaakov, Jewish and Iranian Studies in Honor of Yaakov Elman*. Leiden and Boston: E.J. Brill.
Shaked, Shaul. 2016. "Jews in Khorasan before the Mongol invasion," in *Iran Namag*, edited by Nahid Pirnazar, vol. 1, no .2.
Soroudi, Sarah. 1982, "Shirā-ye Hatani, A Judeo-Persian Wedding Song, " in *Irano-Judaica*, vol. 1. Jerusalem: Ben Zvi Institute.
Spuler, B. 1939. Die Mongolen in Iran, Leipzig.
Stanford Encyclopedia of Philosophy S.V. "ibn-kammuna". https://plato.stanford.edu/entries/ibn-kammuna/
Tadmor, H. 1976. "The Babylonian Exile, and the Restoration," in *History of Jewish People*, edited by Haiym. H. Ben Sasson, 171–172. Cambridge: Harvard University Press.
Turkaman. Eskandar Beig, 1382/2003. *Tarikh-e 'Alamaray-e 'Abbasi*. 2 volumes, edited by Iraj Afshar Tehran: Amir Kabir.
"The Yahuds". 1901. In *Dabistān al Mazāheb (School of Manners)*. Translated into English by David Shea and Anthony Troyer. Introduction by A.V. Williams Jackson. Washington and London: M. Walter Dunnel.
Yeroushalmi, David. 2011. "Amnon Netzer," in *The History of Contemporary Iranian Jews*, edited by Houman Sarshar. Beverly Hills: Center for Iranian Jewish Oral History.
———. 1995. *The Judeo-Persian Poet 'Emrani and His Book of Treasure, Ganjnameh, a Versified Commentary on the Mishnaic Tractate Abot*, vol. 5. Leiden, New York, and Koln: E.J. Brill.
Zhang, Zhan. 2010. *Irano-Judaica*, Conference, Jerusalem.

Index

Note: Page numbers in italic indicate a figure and page numbers in bold indicate a table on the corresponding page.

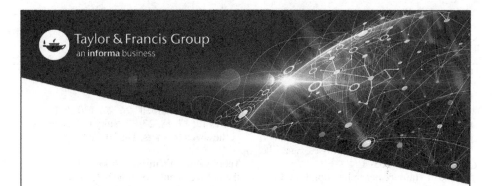

9781032145761